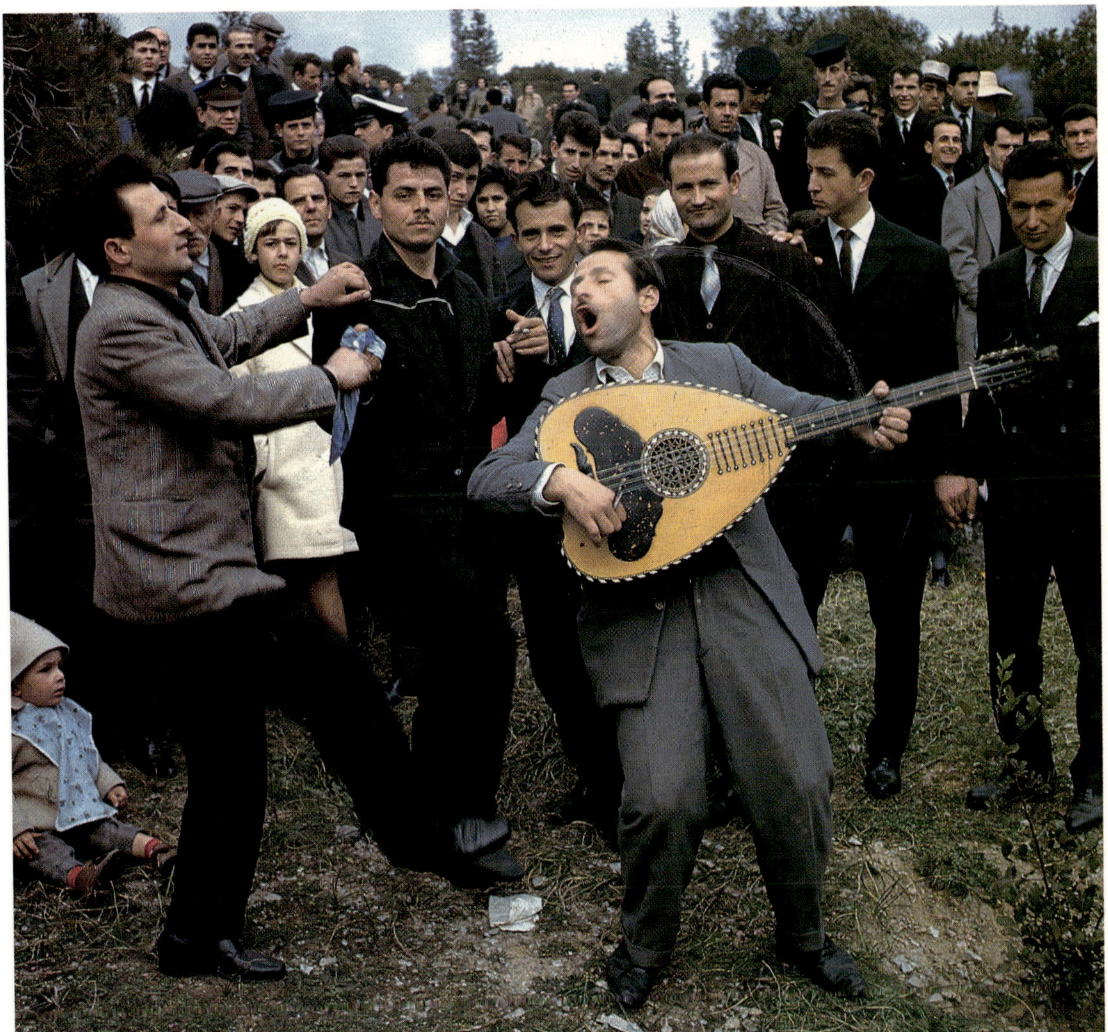

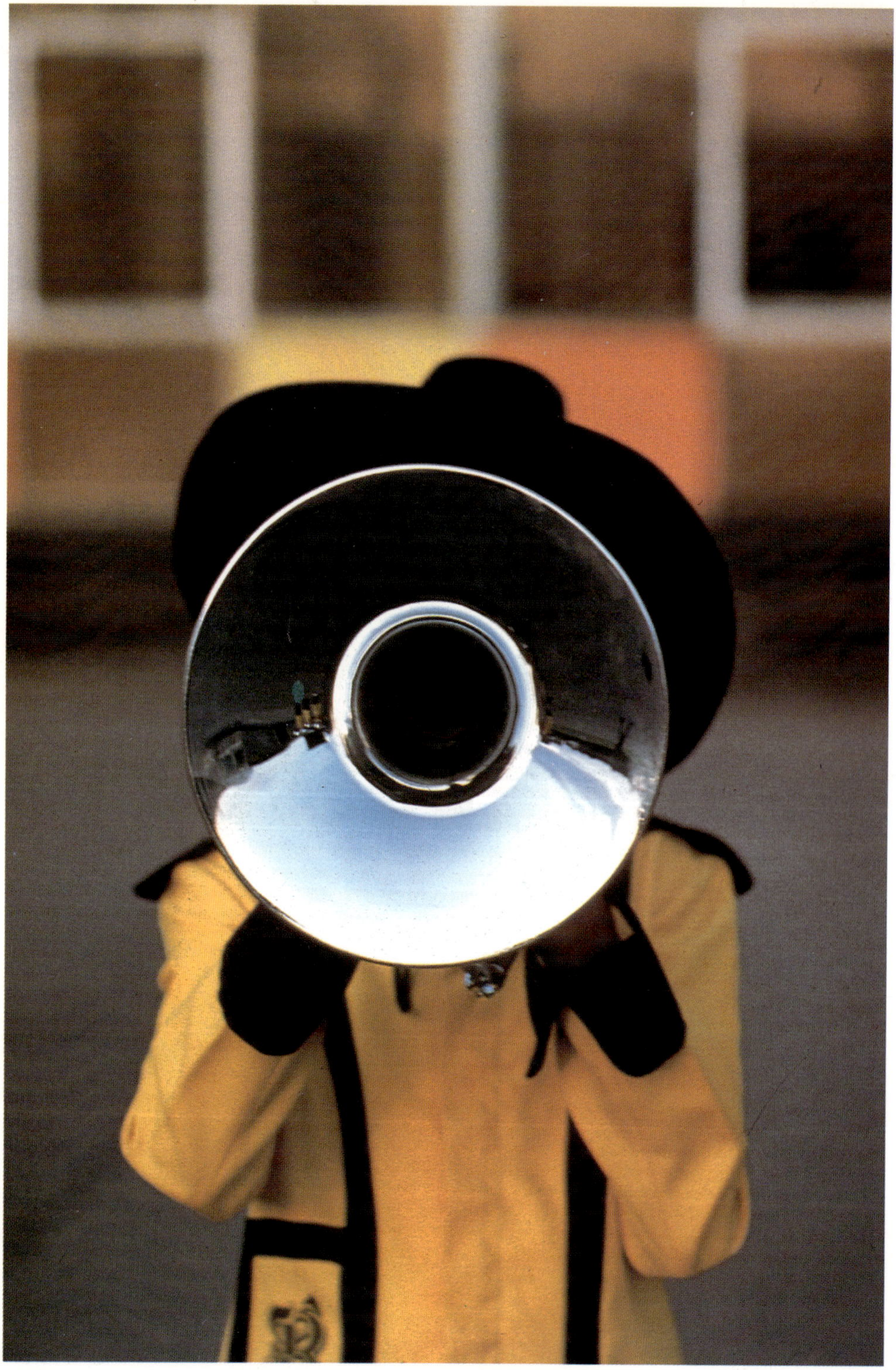

MAGNUM *Images*

MUSIC

André Deutsch

First published in Great Britain in 1990
by André Deutsch Limited
105-106 Great Russell Street, London WC1

Printed in Hong Kong
Book design by Michael Rand and Ian Denning.

British Library Cataloguing in Publication Data
Music — (Magnum images).
1. Photographs. Special subjects. Music
I. Magnum Photos II. Series
779.978

ISBN 0-233-98605-7

Printed in Hong Kong by
Dah Hua Printing Press Co., Ltd.

Introduction

Magnum, the great photographic co-operative, was founded in 1947, although a number of its members had been taking superb photographs since the Thirties. In this book Magnum presents a dazzling selection of some of the finest images devoted to the celebration of music in all its forms.

MUSIC contains an extraordinary variety of images, some of great performers ranging from The Beatles to Maria Callas, Pablo Casals to Jacqueline du Pré, Charlie Parker, Louis Armstrong, Isaac Stern, Vladimir Horowitz . . .

But music is also shown in its many guises, from an unknown Chinese listening to a canary to a Japanese robot playing an organ.

There are violins, Scottish bagpipes, Greek bouzoukia, British marching bands, Indian sitar players, Nuba tribal musicians, a Polish funeral band and a New Orleans funeral jazz band.

Above all music is shown as an extraordinary celebration, from individual virtuosi to music practised in vast numbers. There is a rock festival on the Isle of Wight, alpine horn blowing in Switzerland, the Boston Symphony Orchestra playing with the Beijing Symphony Orchestra.

The images gathered here represent a unique celebration of one of man's greatest joys.

Cover
Costa Manos
Bouzouki player,
Greece, 1985.

Frontispiece
Peter Marlow
Marching Band,
Birmingham,
England, 1984.

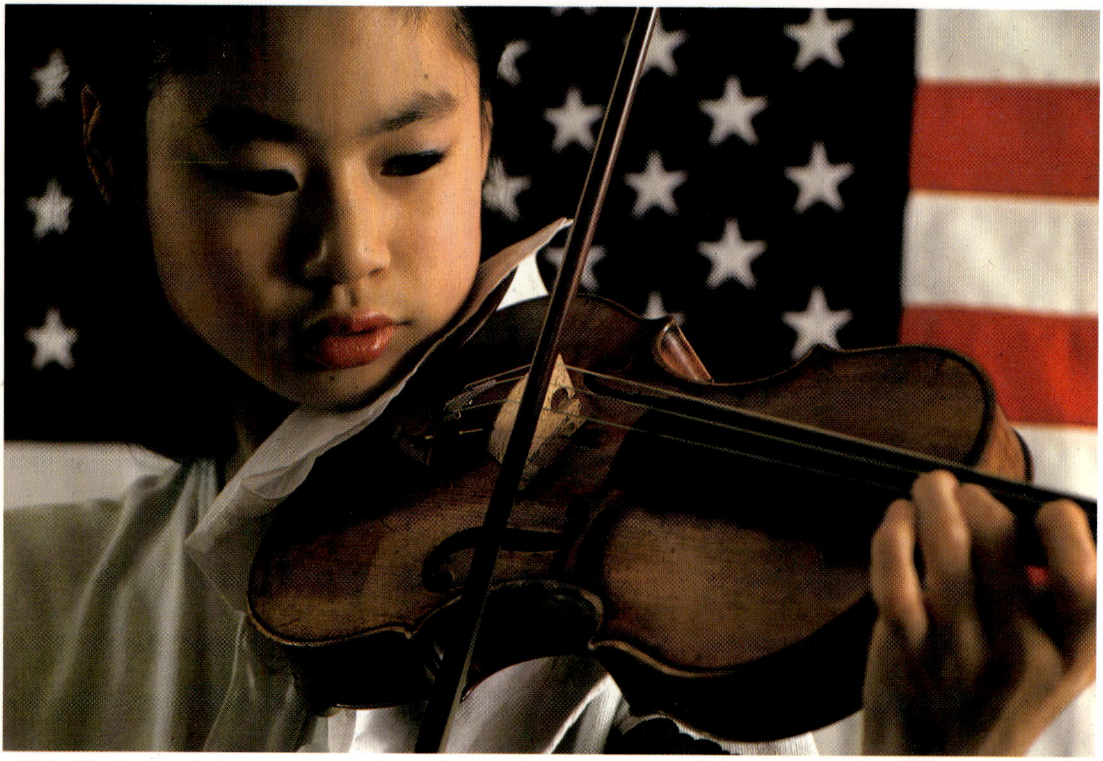

Erich Hartmann
Midori, 16 year-old Japanese violinist, USA, 1987.

Marc Riboud
Sitar player, India, 1956.

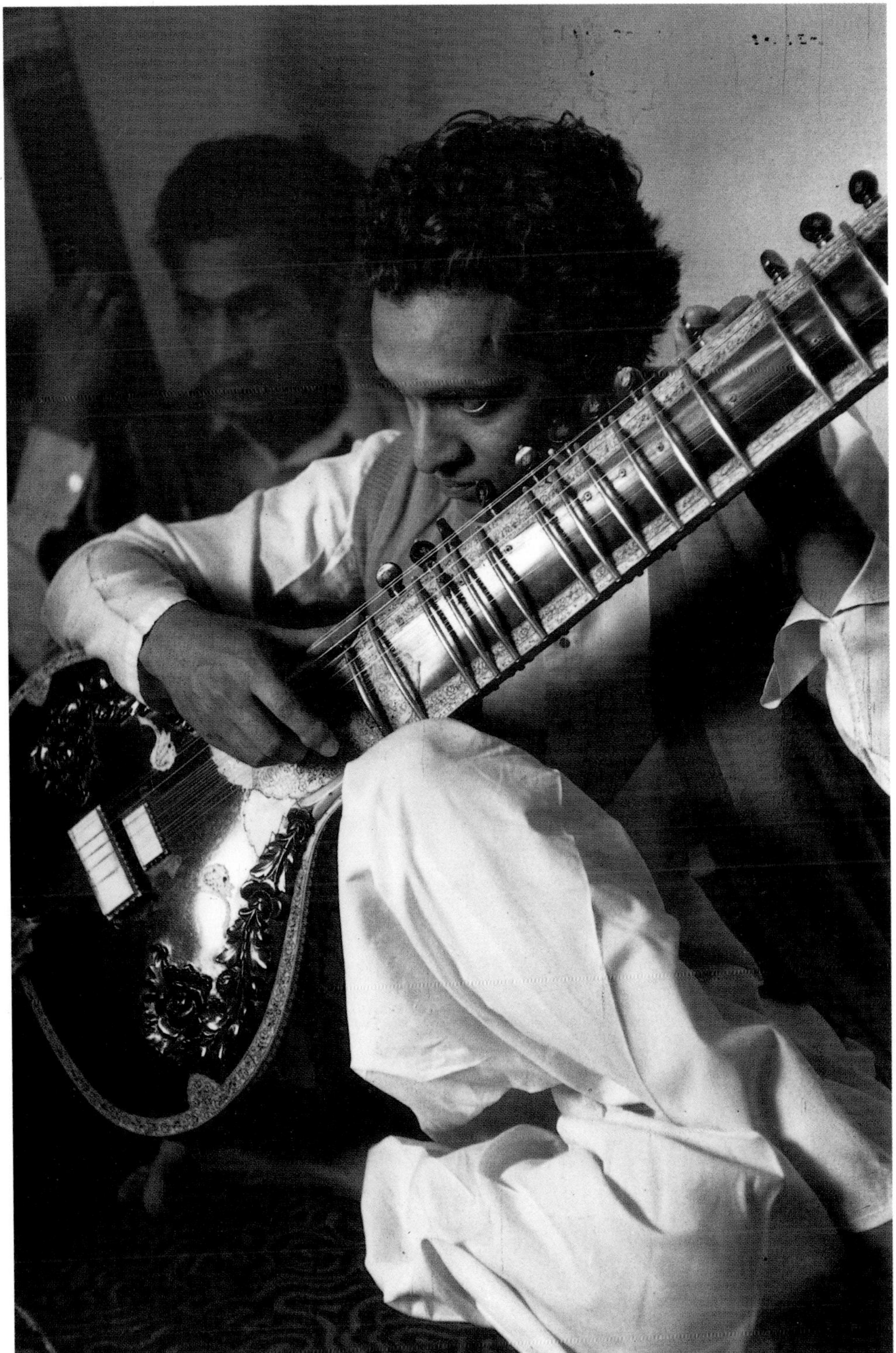

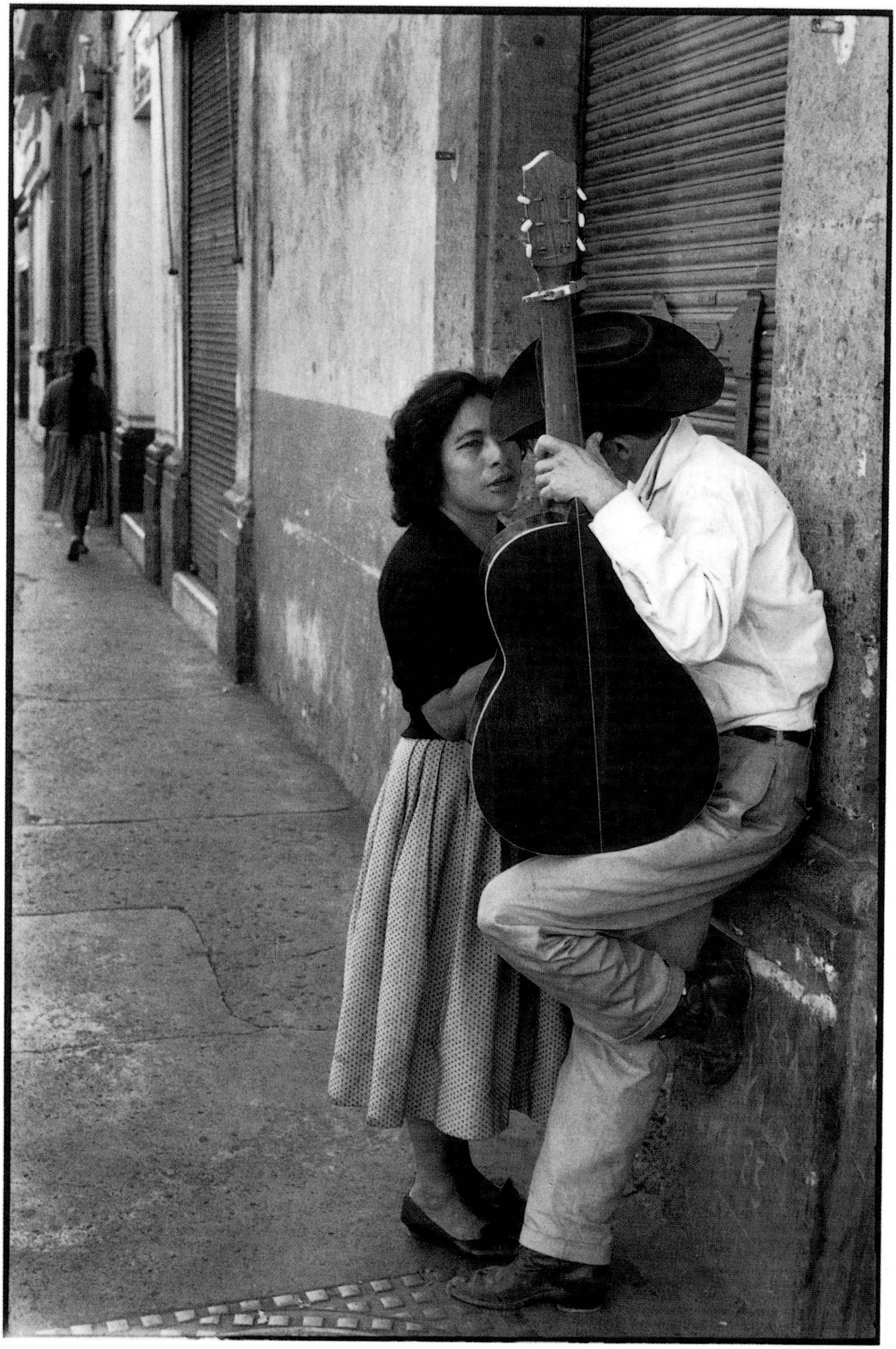

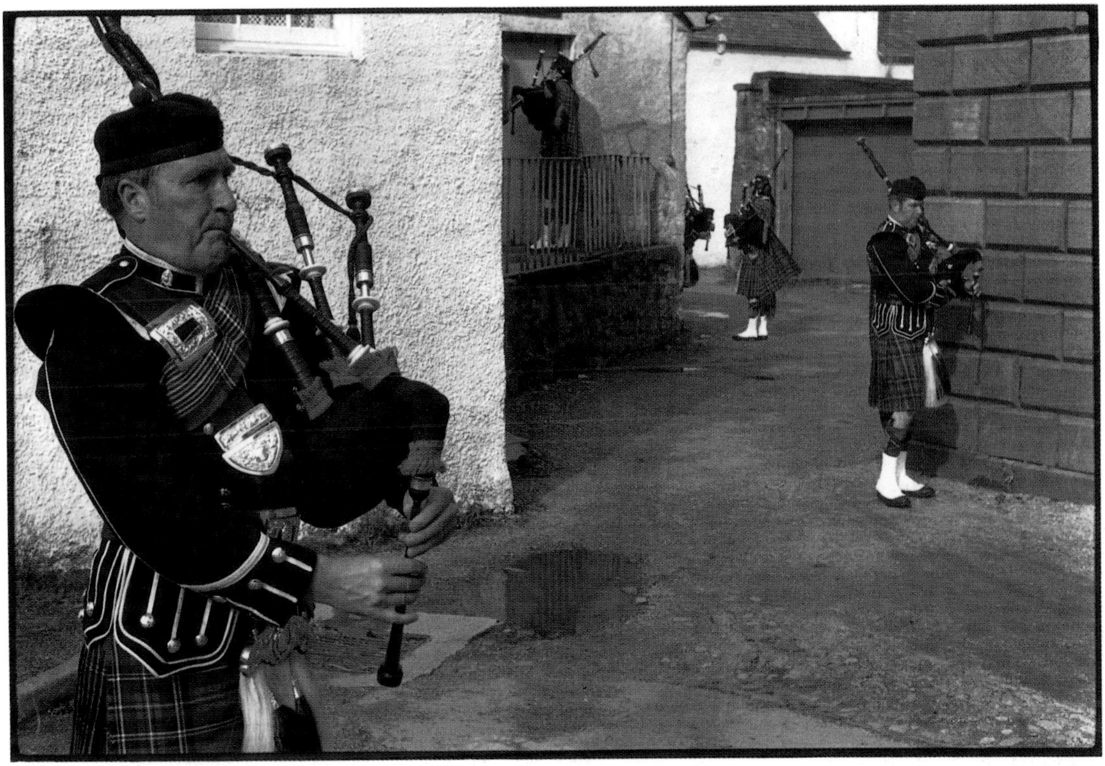

Josef Koudelka
Bagpipers,
UK, 1977.

Henri Cartier-Bresson
Lovers with guitar,
Mexico.

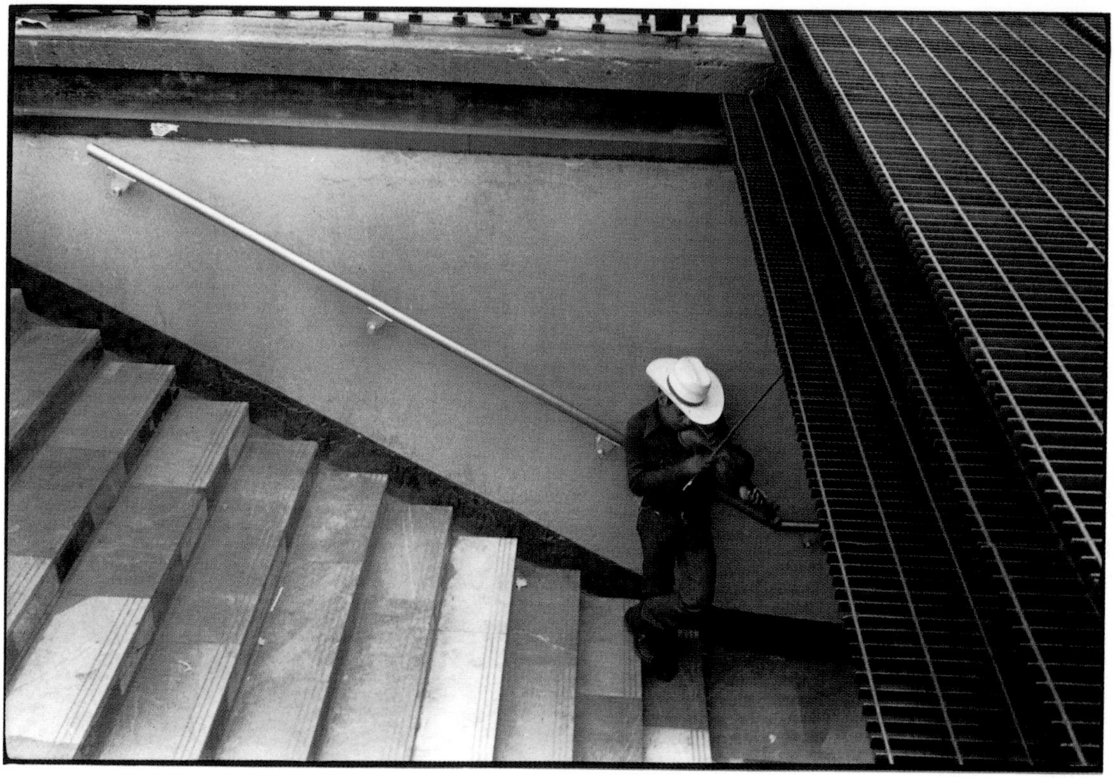

Abbas
Violinist,
Mexico City, 1983.

Erich Hartmann
Kiel Philharmonic,
Germany.

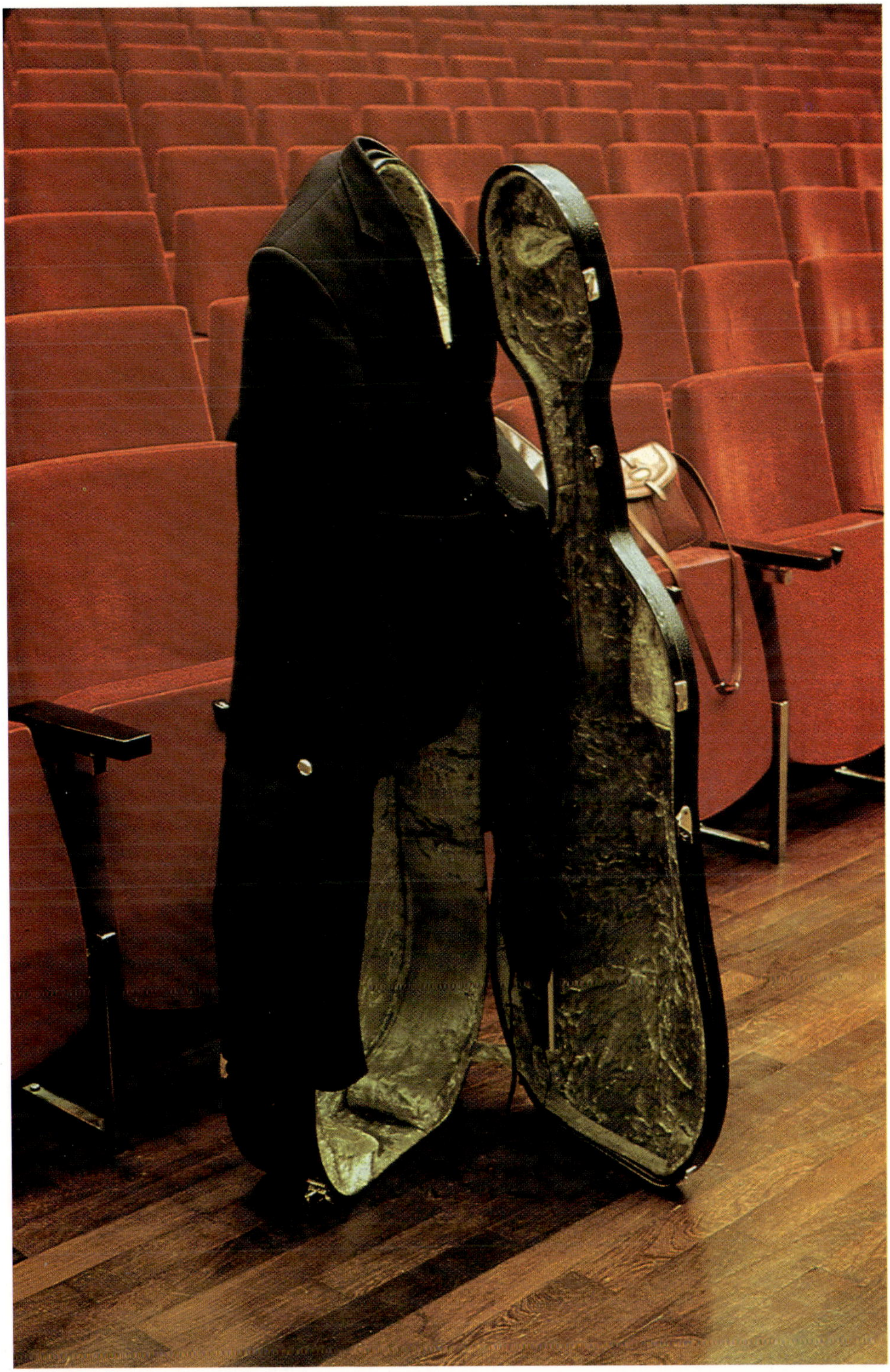

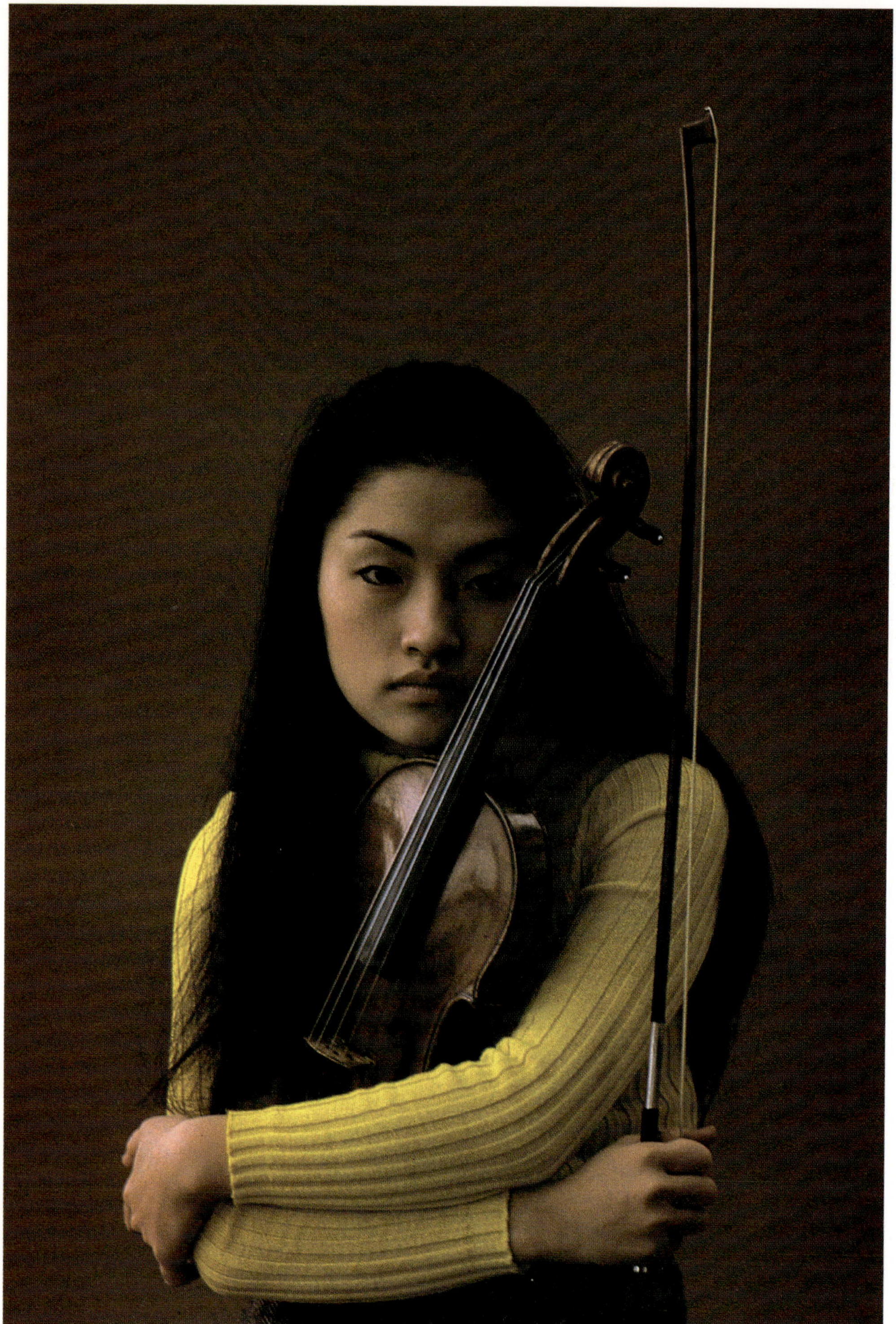

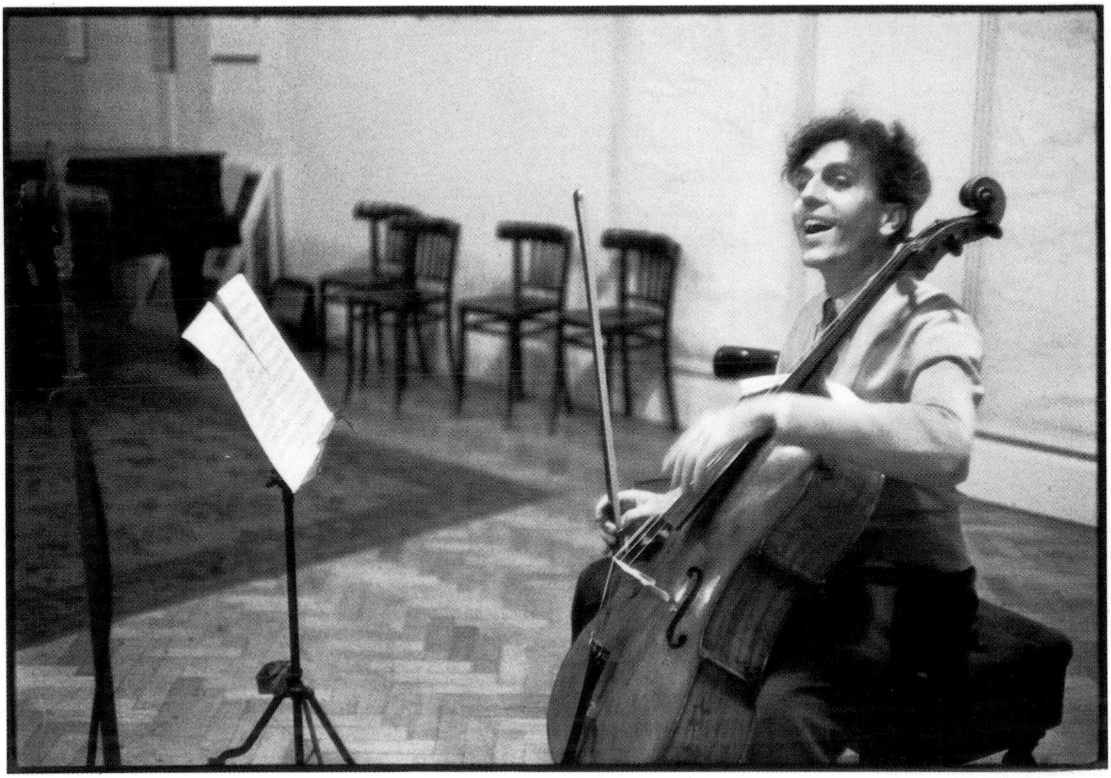

Inge Morath
Paul Tortellier, 1954.

Eve Arnold
Kung Wha Chung, Korean violinist, London, 1970.

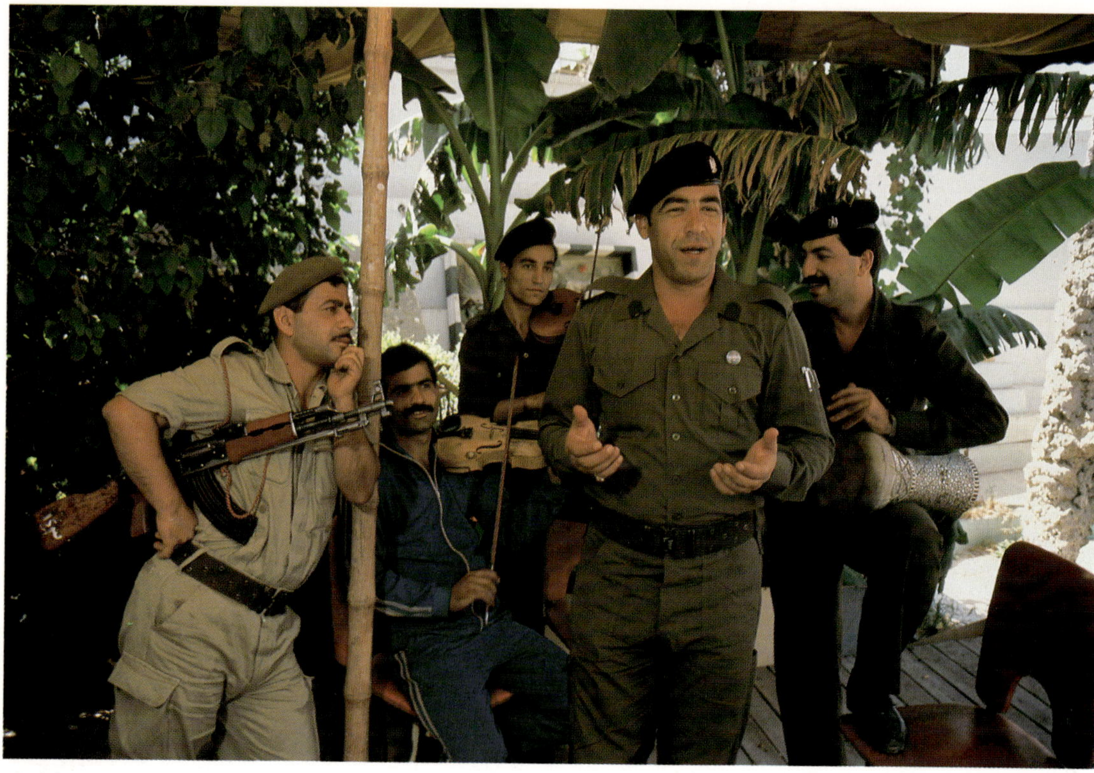

Sebastiao Salgado
Serenading the military,
Iraq, 1983.

Philip Jones-Griffiths
The Beatles on tour,
1961.

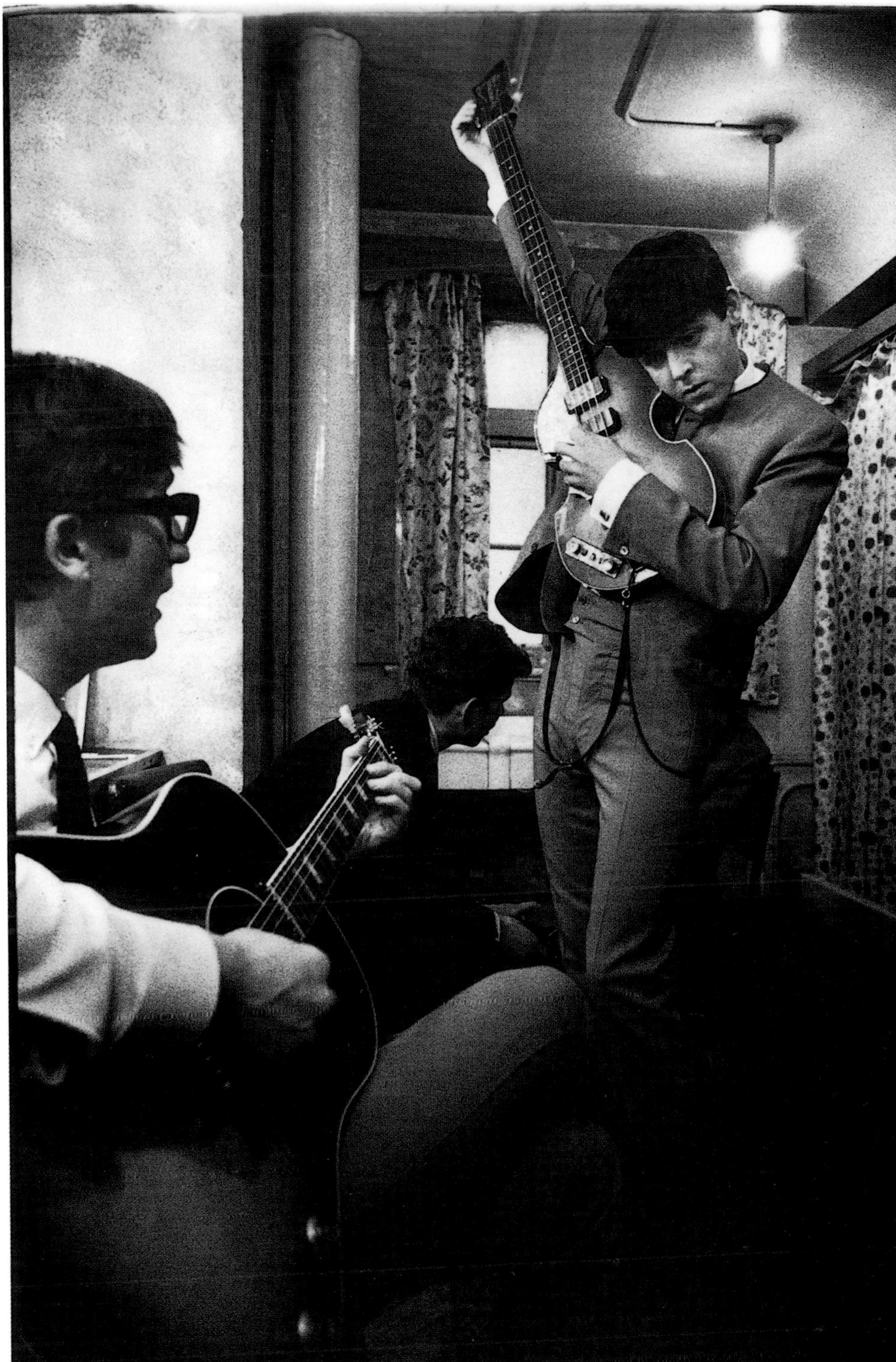

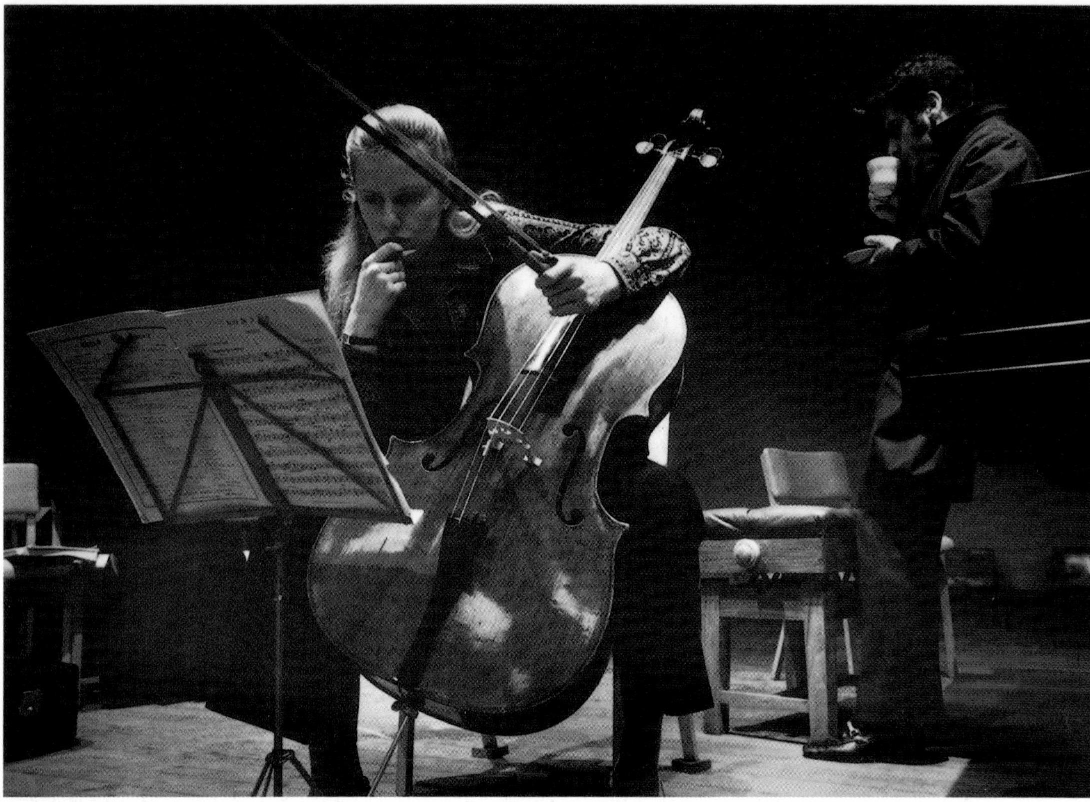

David Hurn
Jacqueline du Pré,
1970.

René Burri
Pablo Casals,
1965.

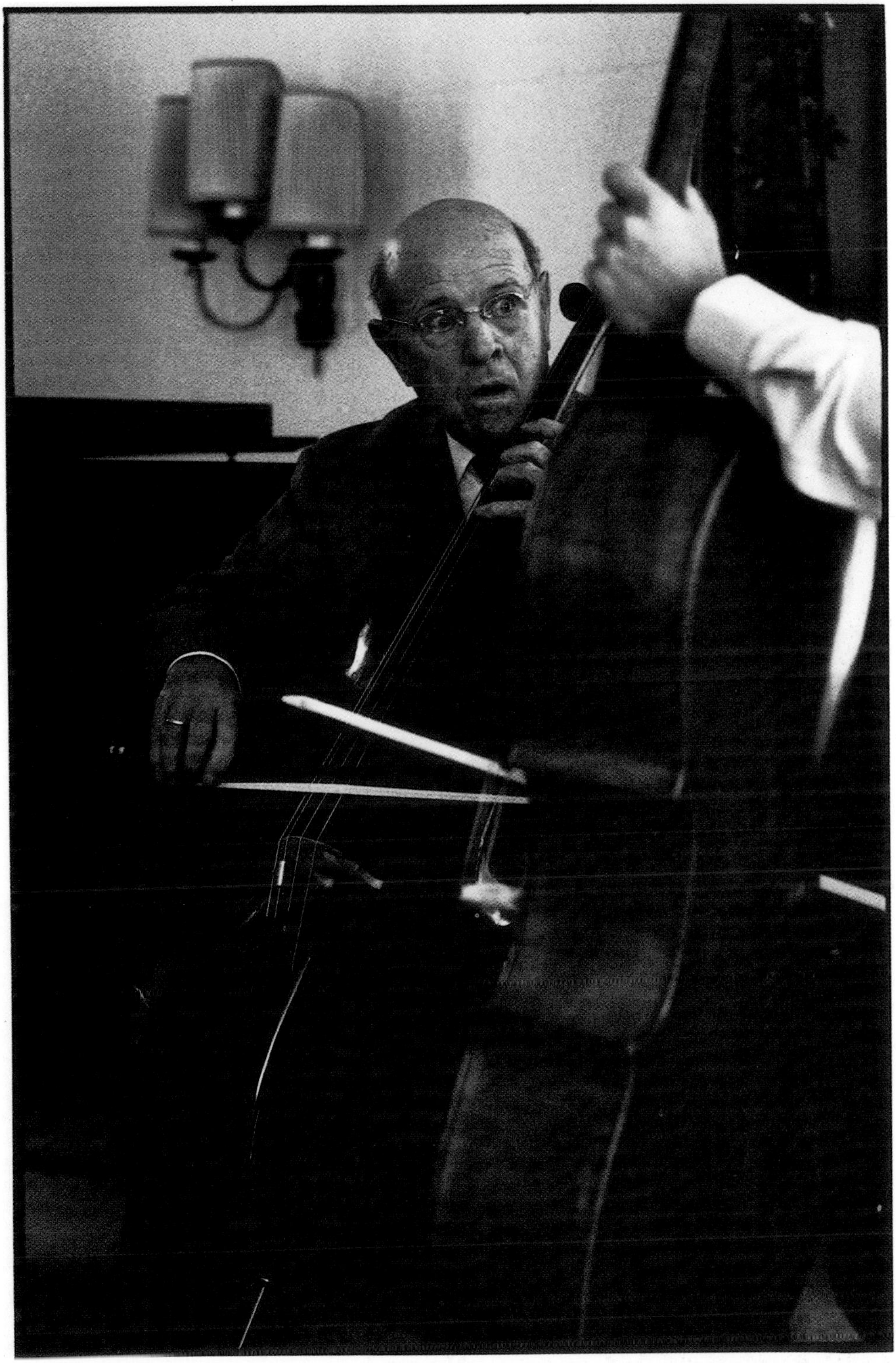

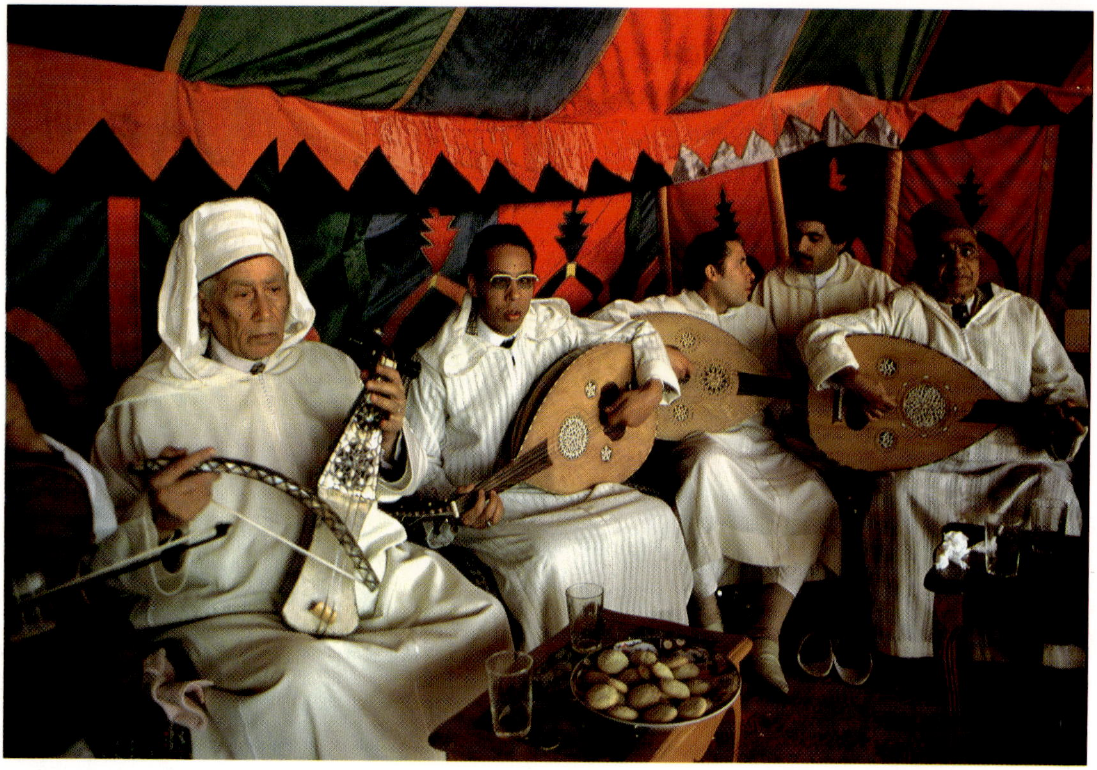

Bruno Barbey
Fez, Morocco,
1986.

Henri Cartier-Bresson
Siena, Italy.

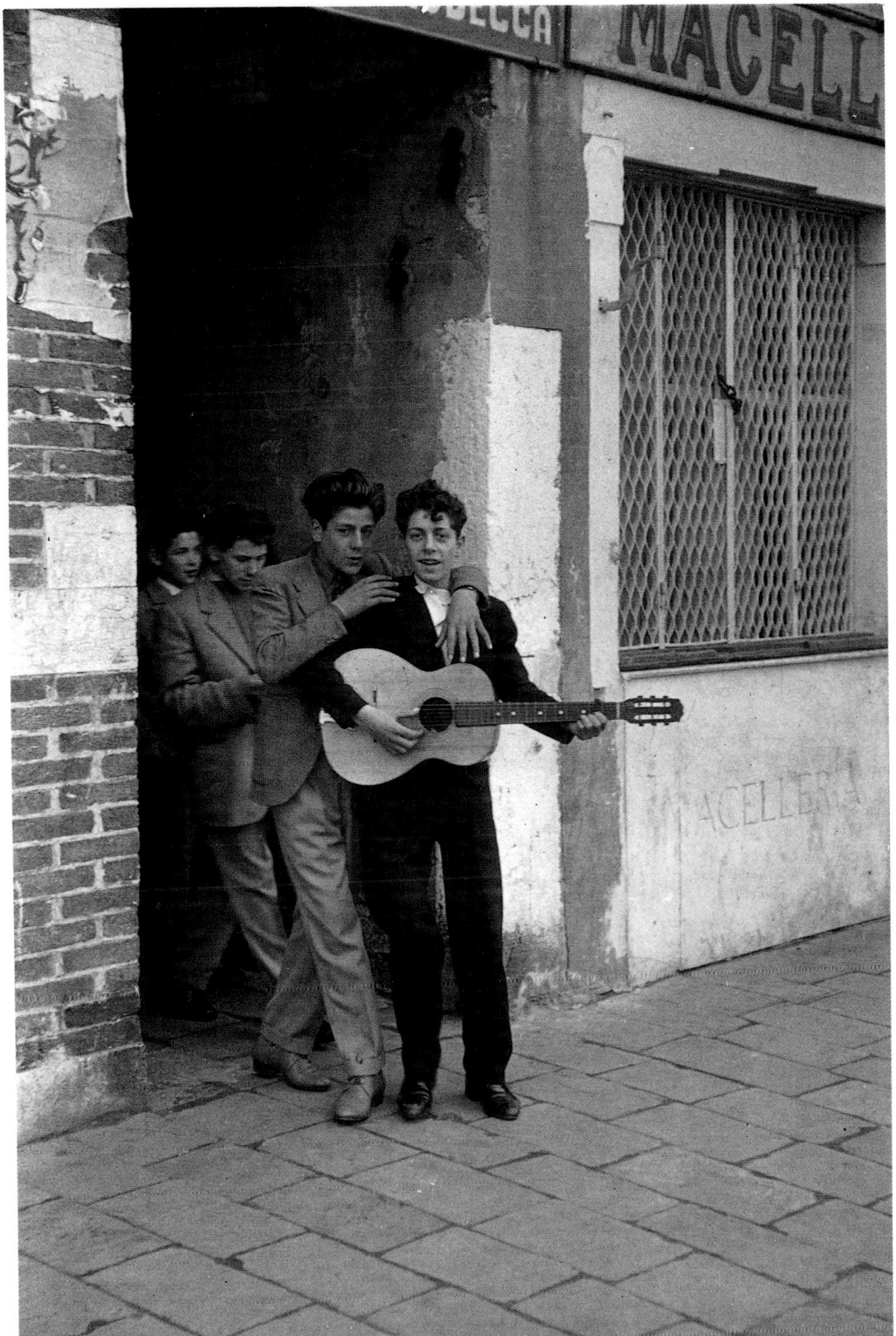
MACELL
MACELLERIA

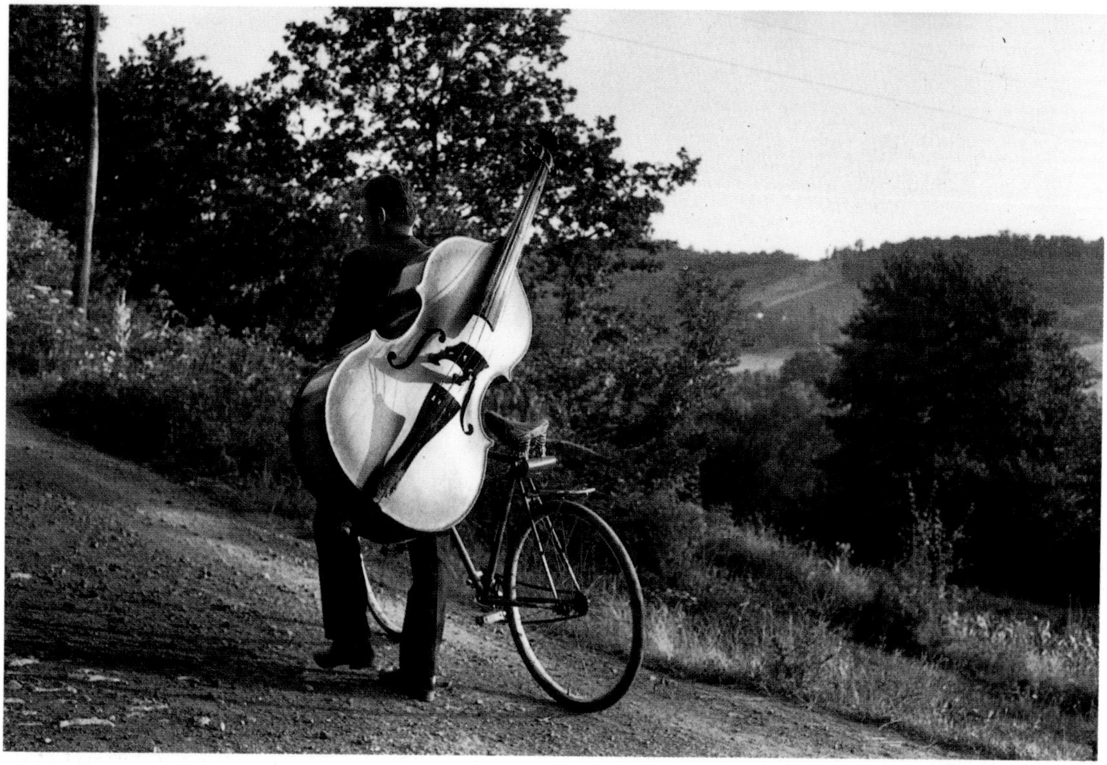

Henri Cartier-Bresson
Slopes of Mt Rudnik, Yugoslavia, 1965.

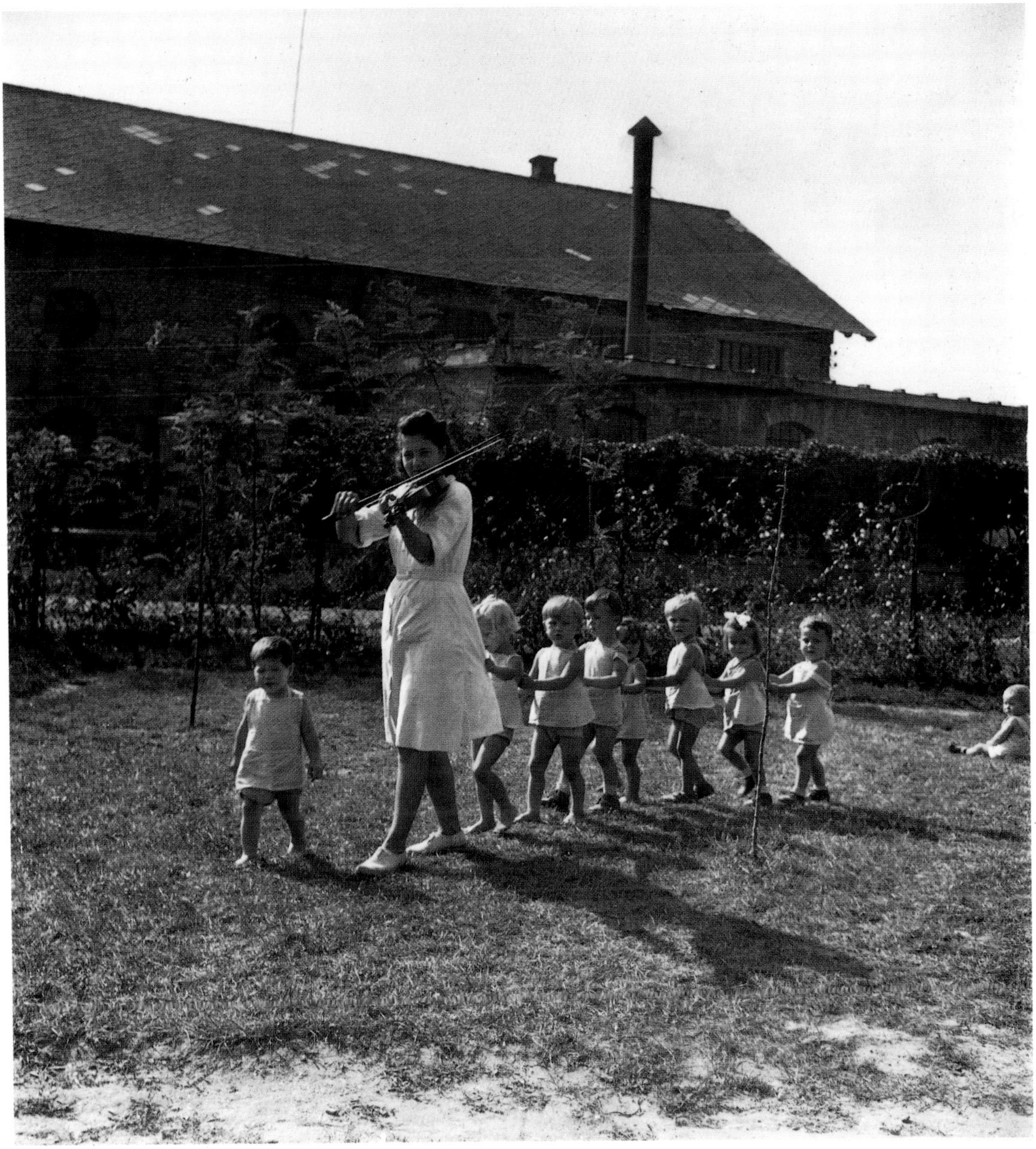

David Seymour
Kindergarten, Vienna.

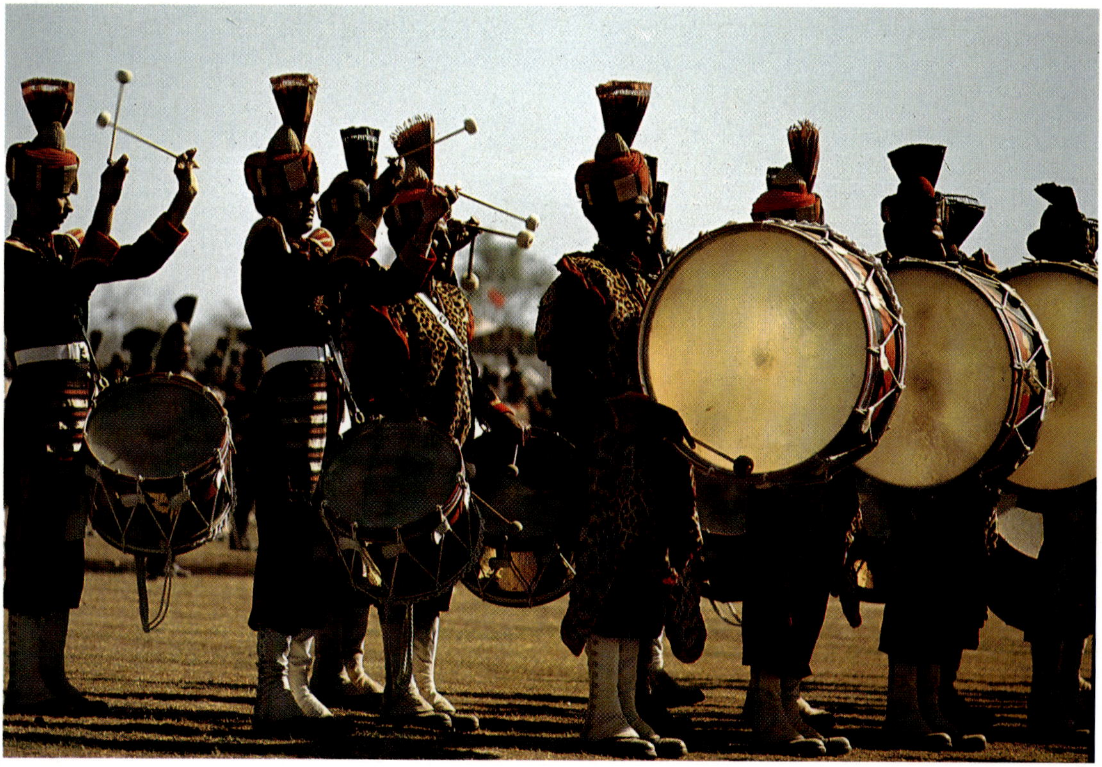

René Burri
Military band, Lahore, Pakistan.

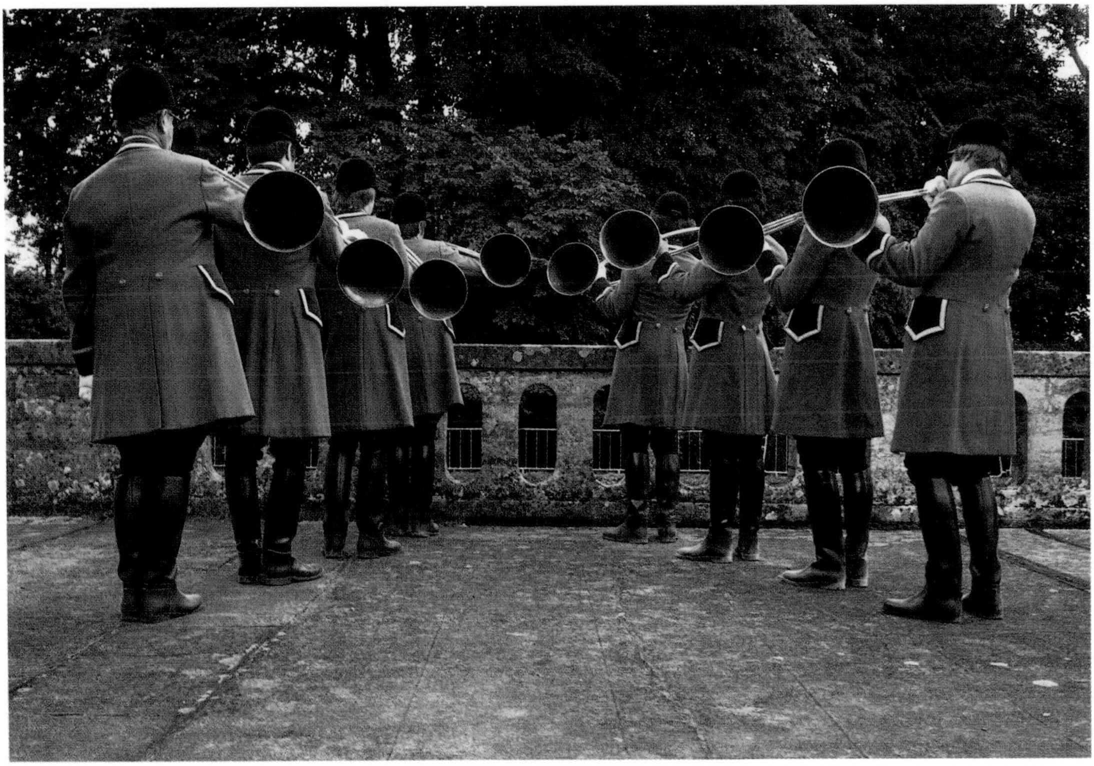

Sebastiao Salgado
Hunting corps at Balleroy, France, 1980.

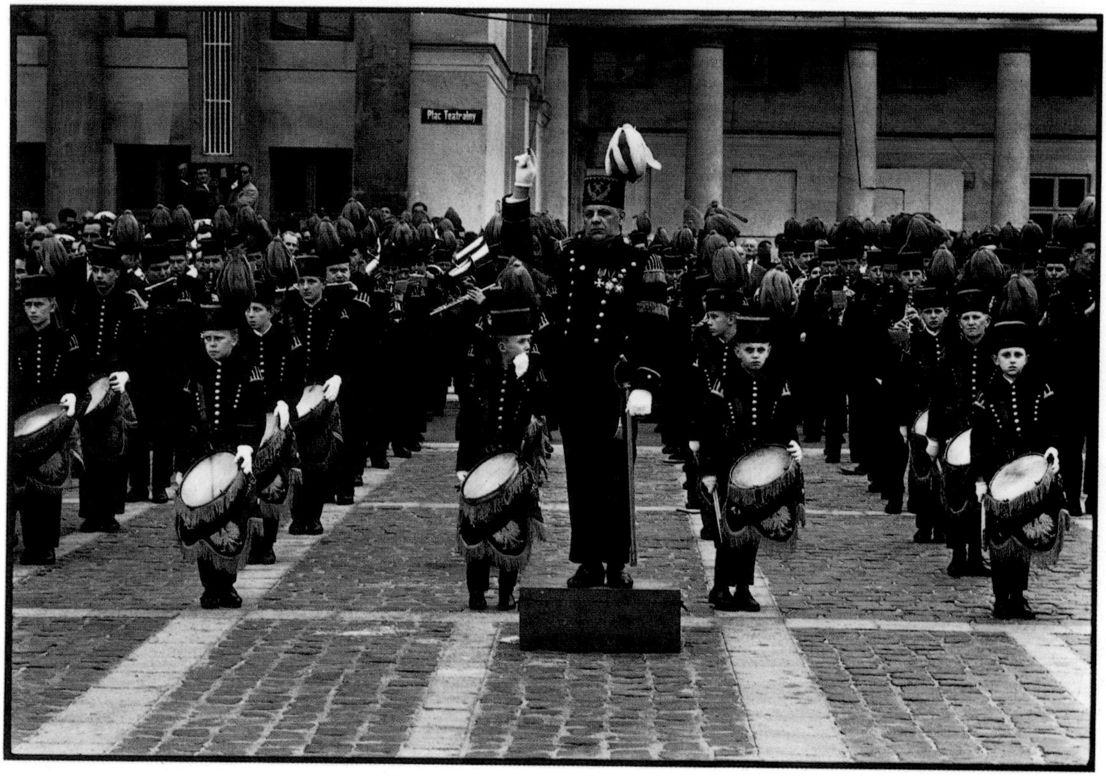

Elliott Erwitt
Funeral band,
Warsaw, 1964.

Martine Franck
Street musicians,
Vaucluse, France.

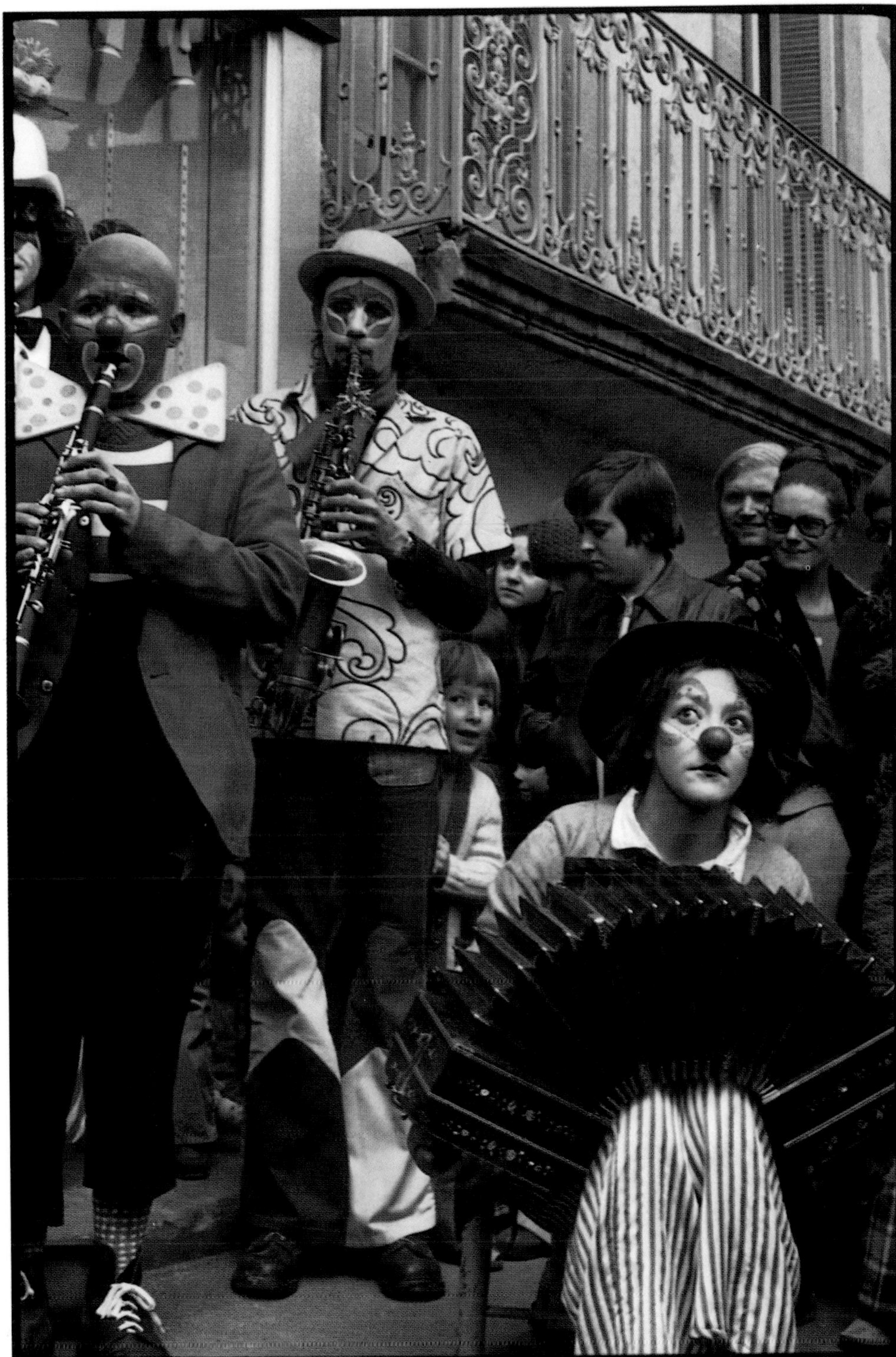

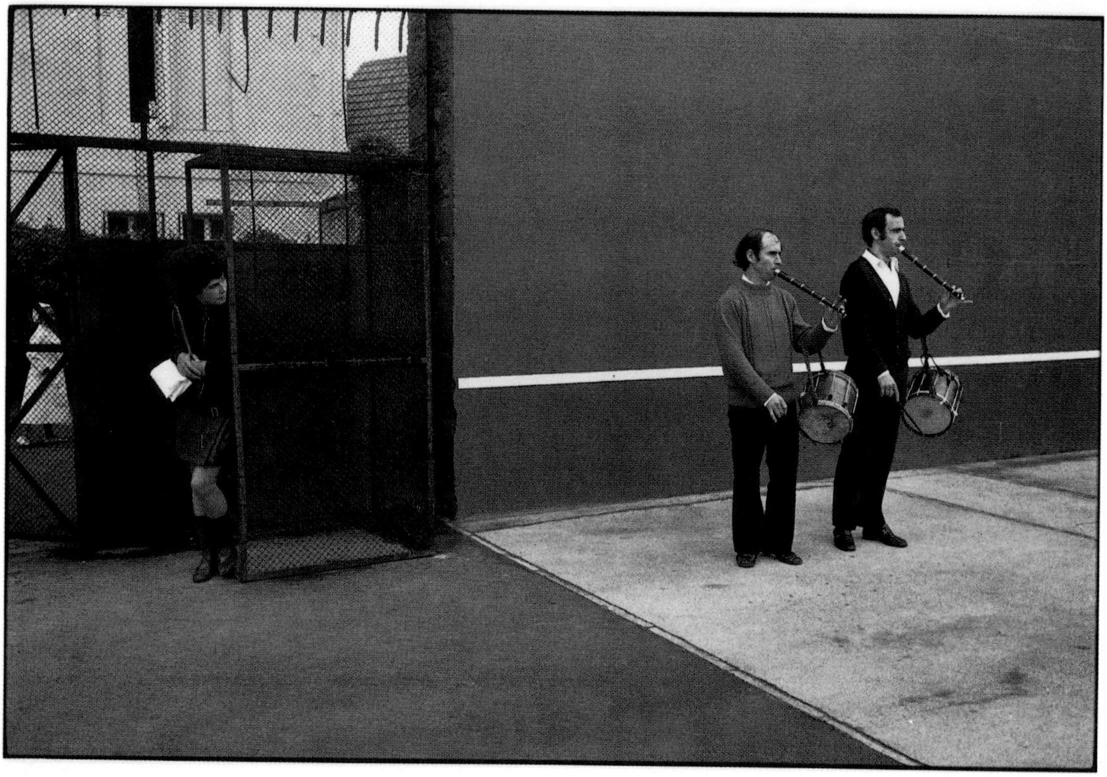

Guy Le Querrec
Biarritz, France,
1971.

René Burri
One-man band, Fifth Avenue,
New York, 1980.

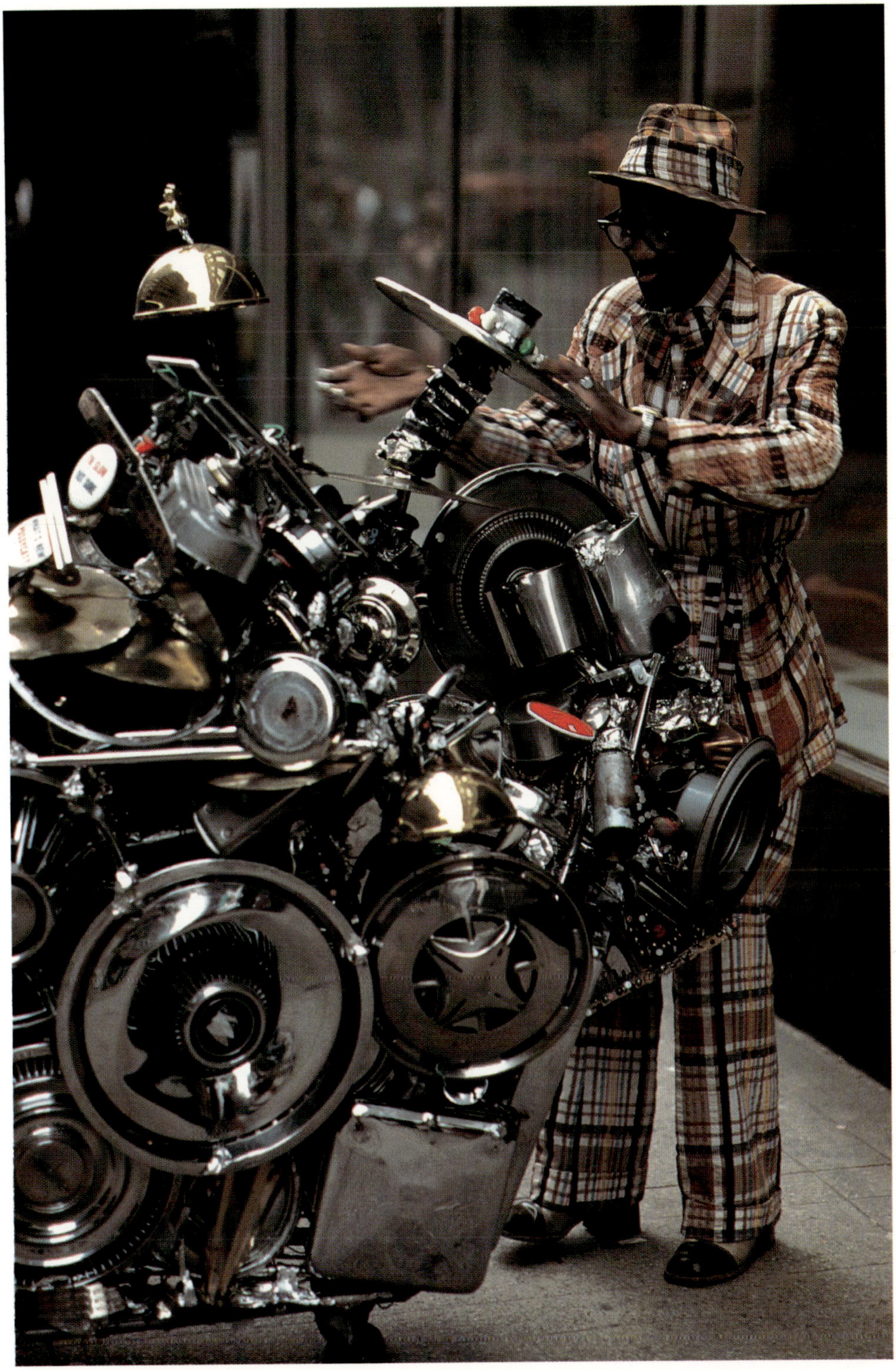

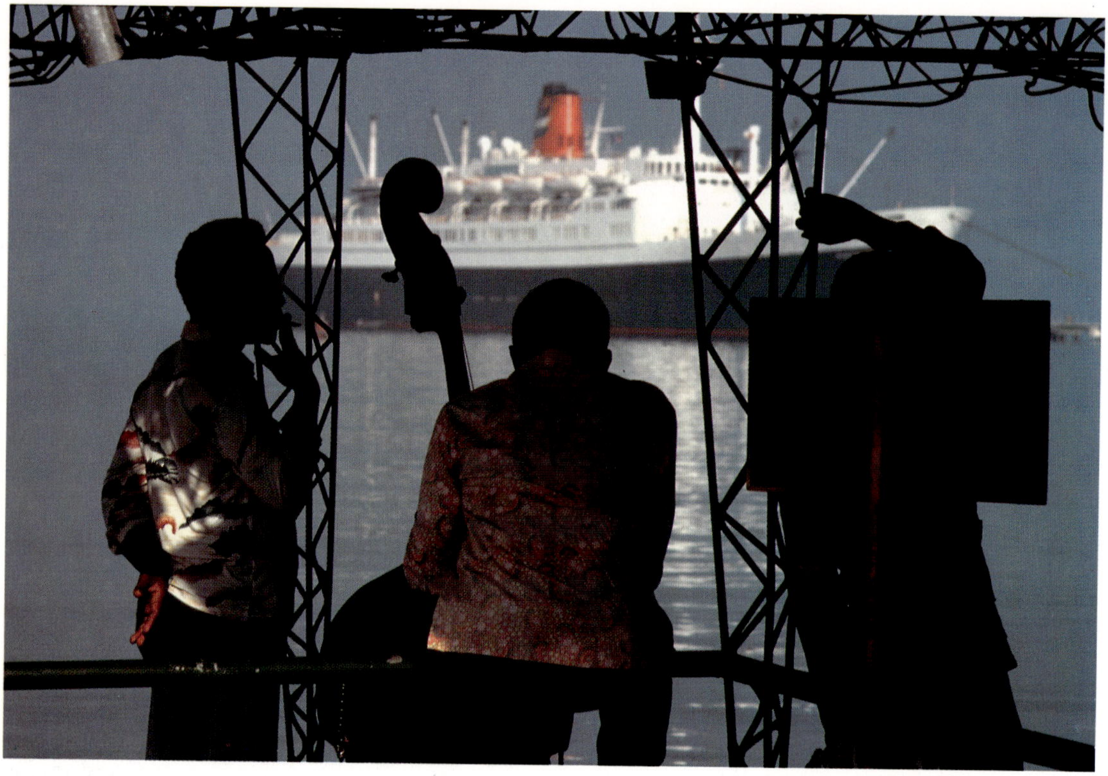

Alex Webb
Haiti, 1987.

Jean Gaumy
Fanfare, Haute Savoie, France, 1978.

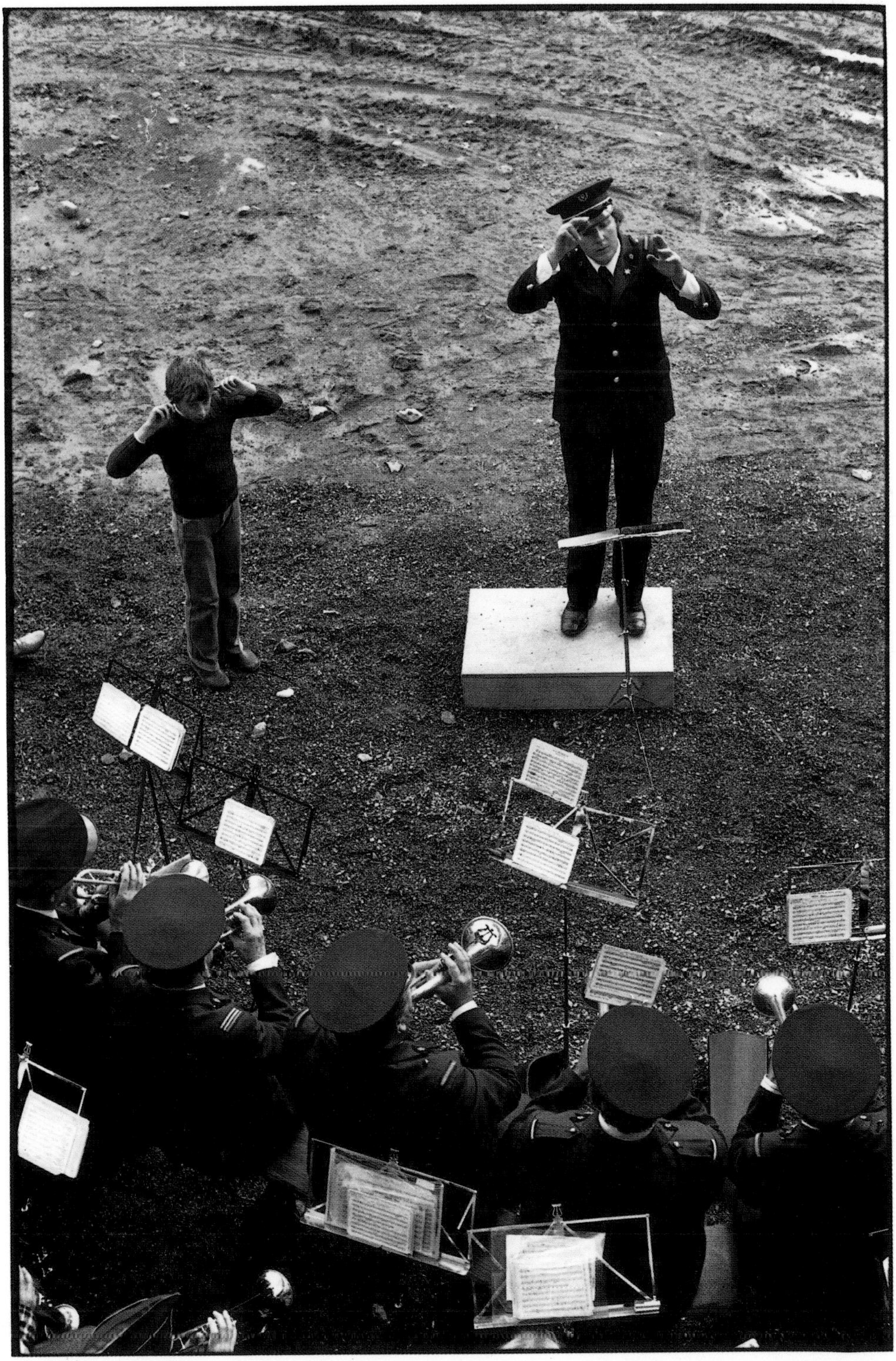

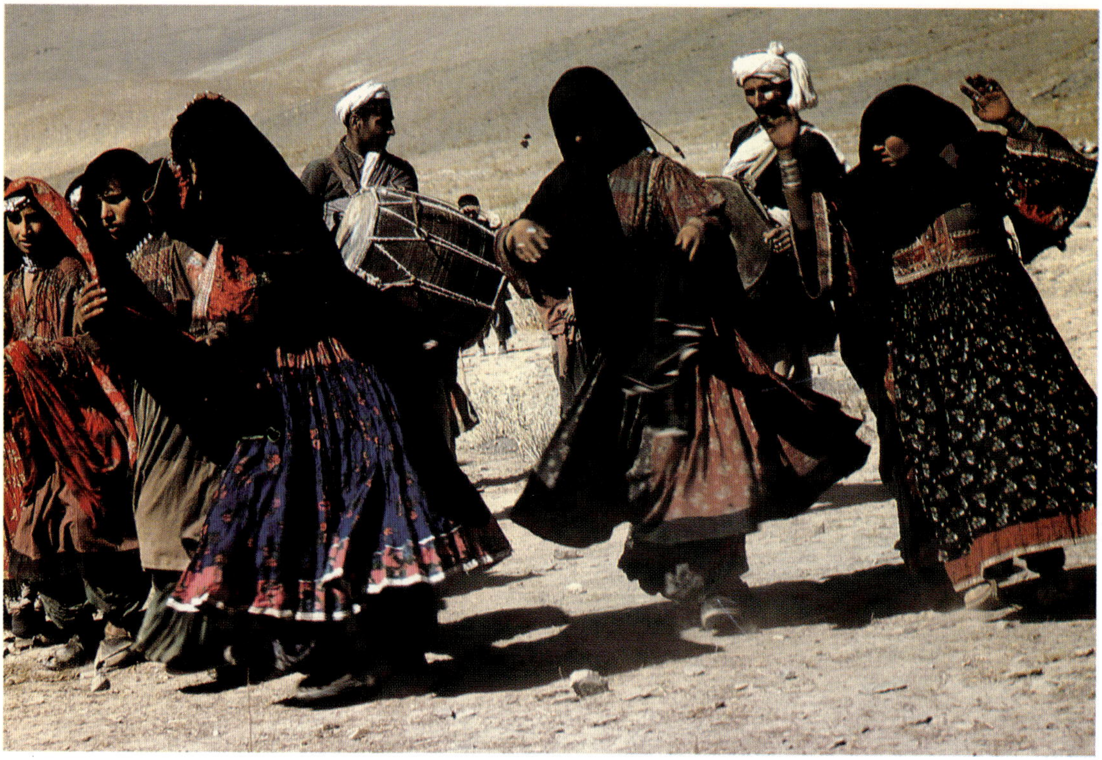

Eve Arnold
Nomad wedding,
Afghanistan, 1969.

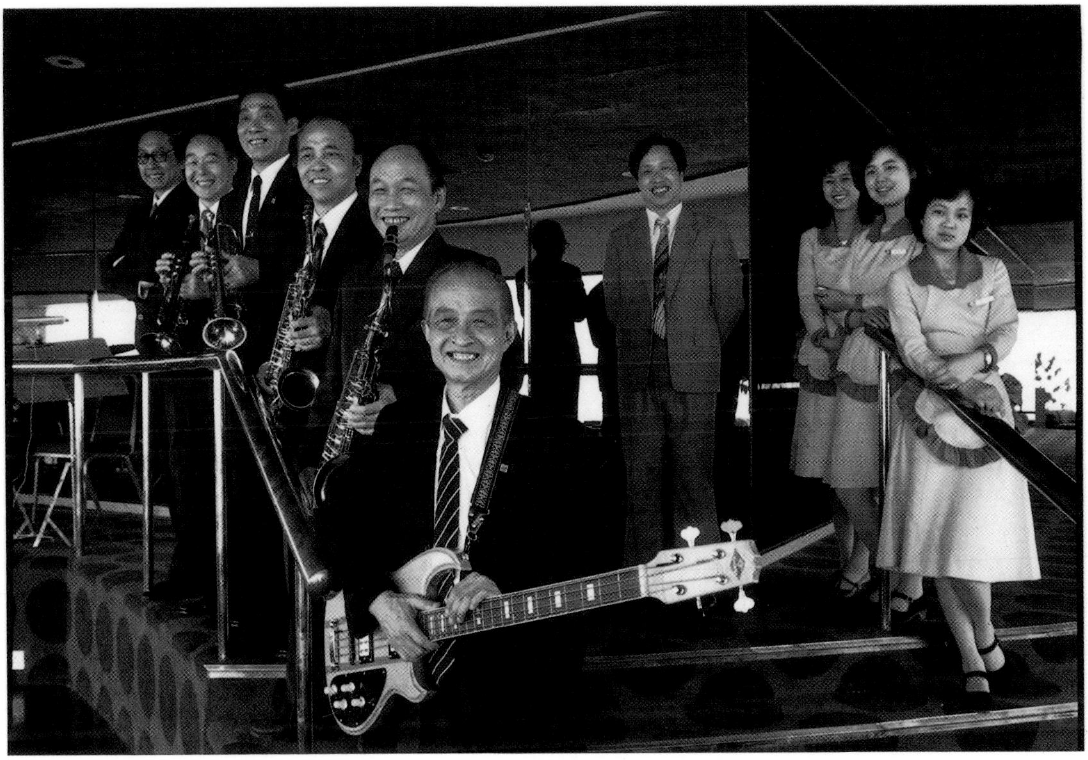

Guy Le Querrec
Jingling Jazz Band,
Nanjing, China, 1980.

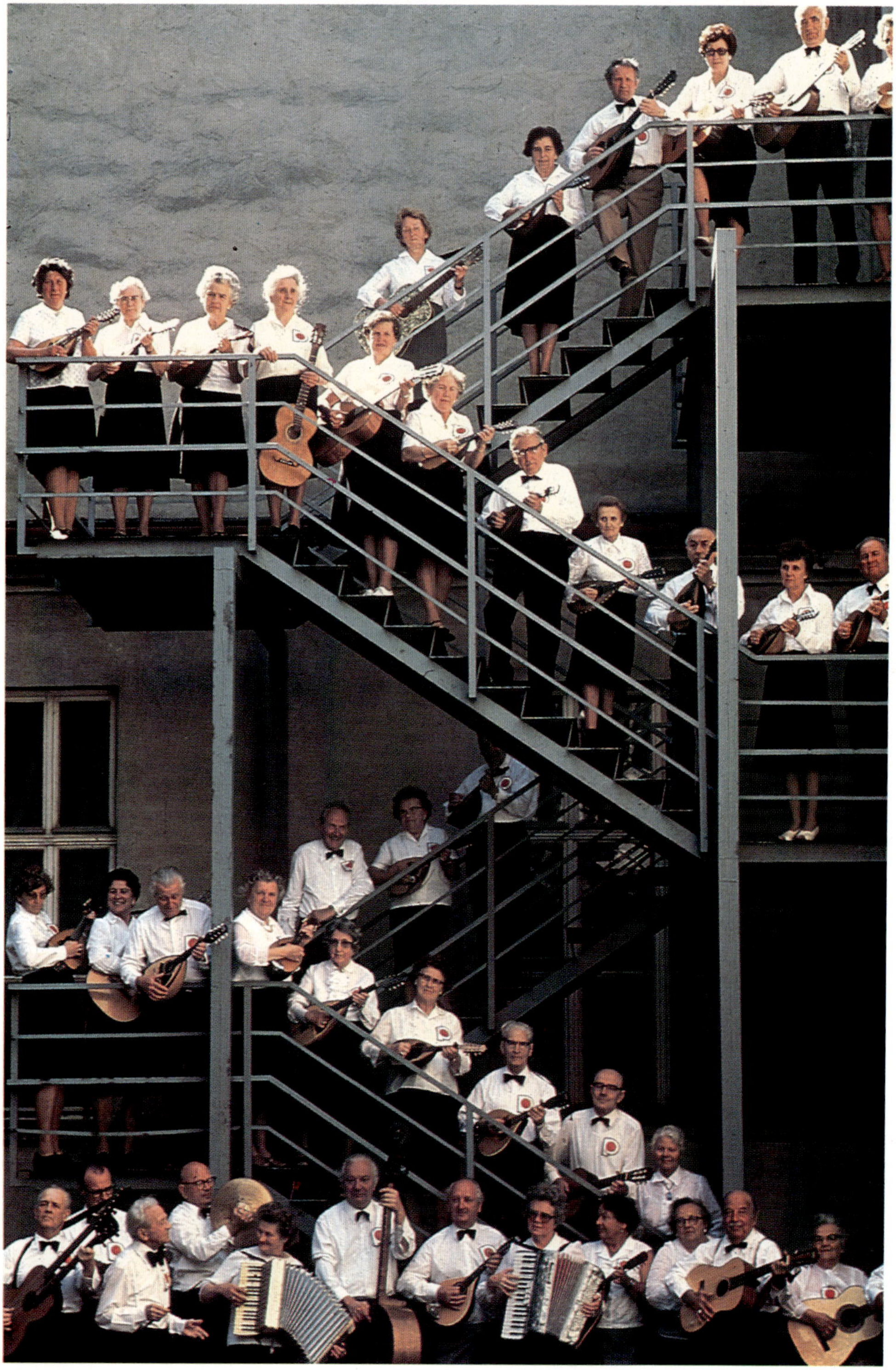

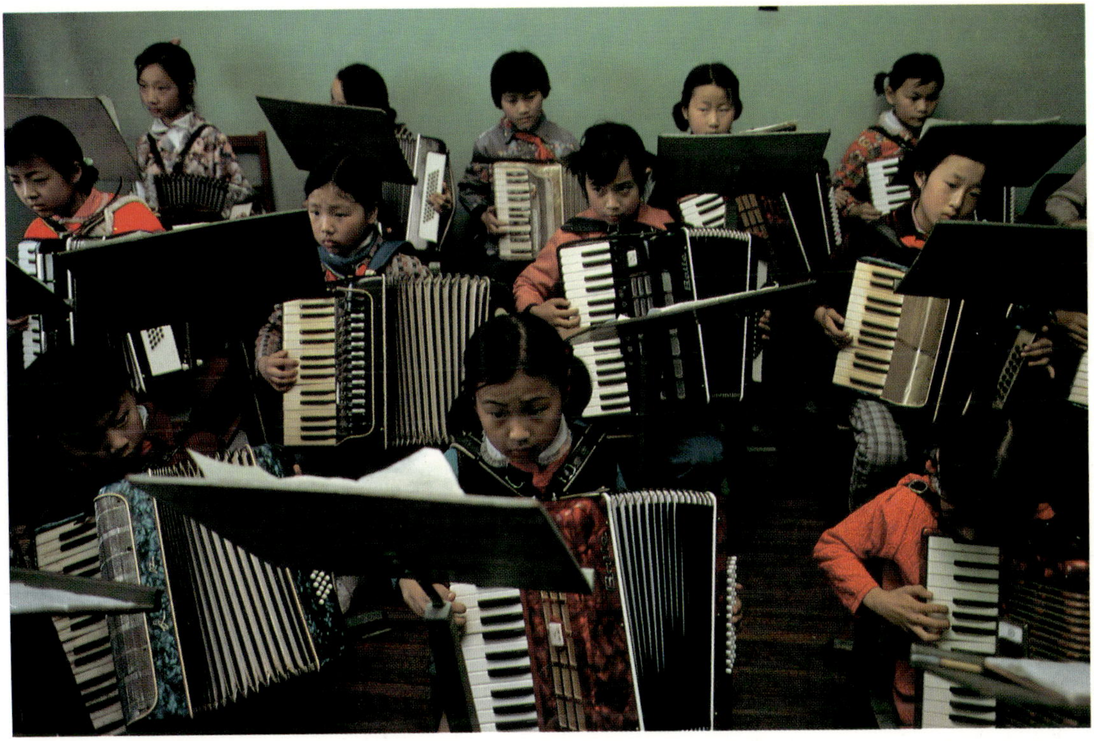

Bruno Barbey
Shanghai, China, 1980.

Thomas Hoepker
Pensioners' orchestra, Vienna, 1978.

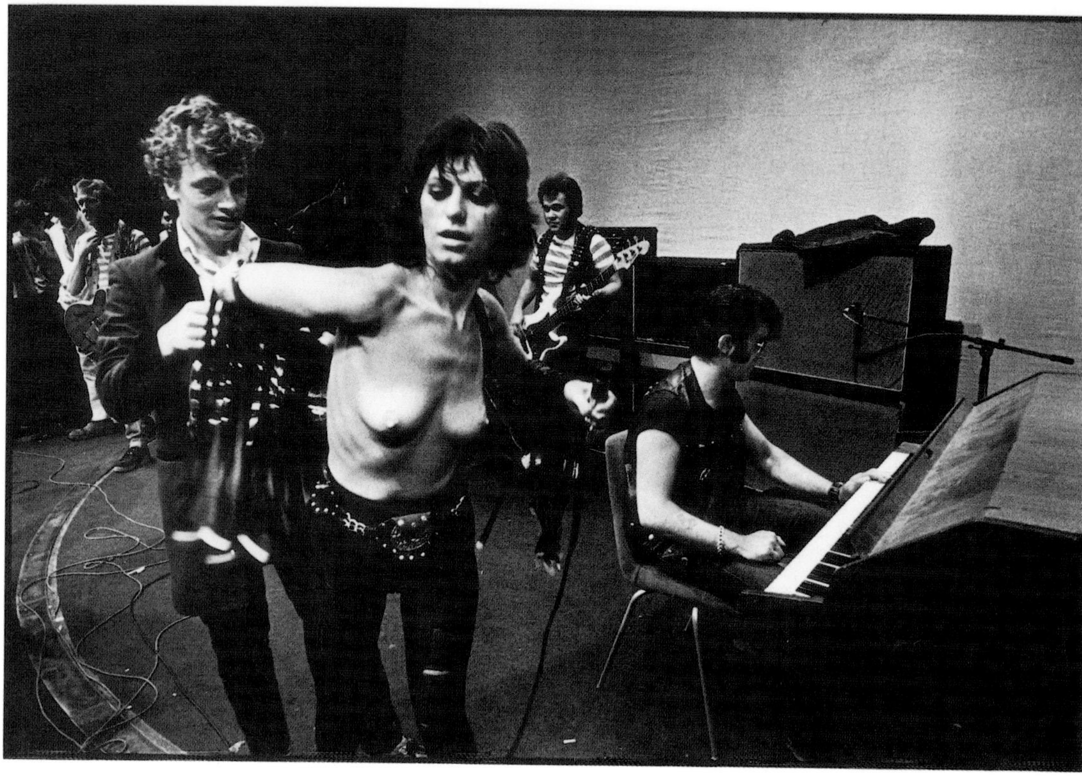

Chris Steele-Perkins
Teddy boy concert, Lyceum Ballroom, London, 1976.

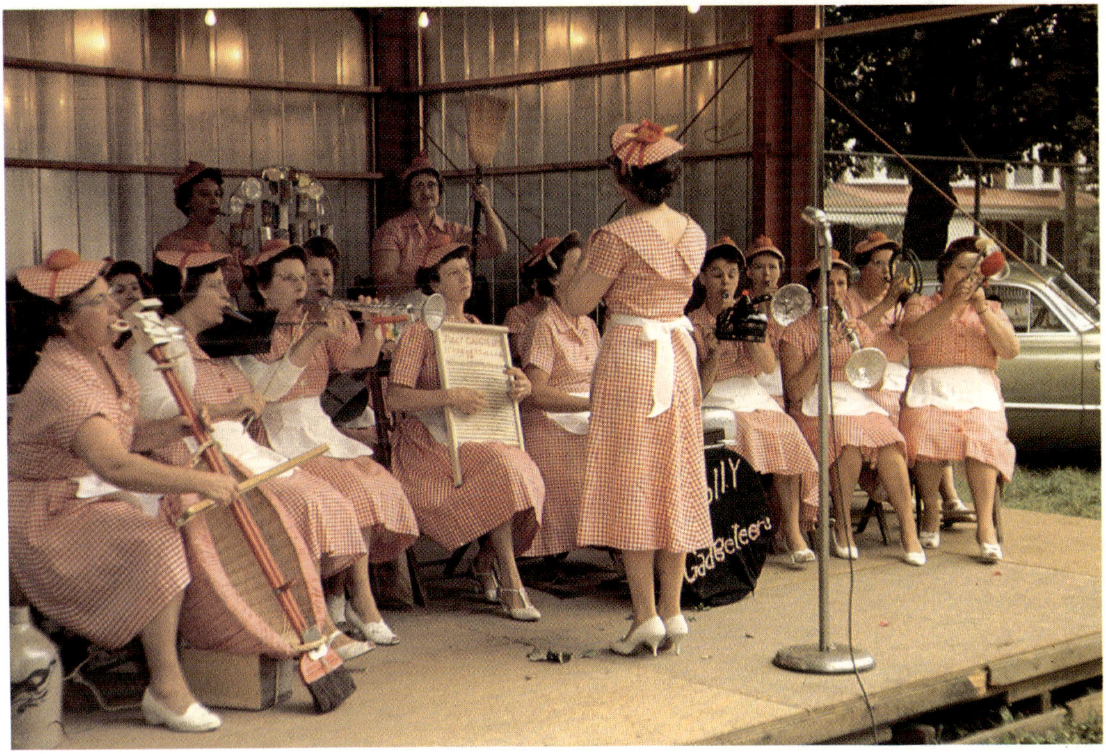

Dennis Stock
Women's band, Allentown, Pennsylvania, 1961.

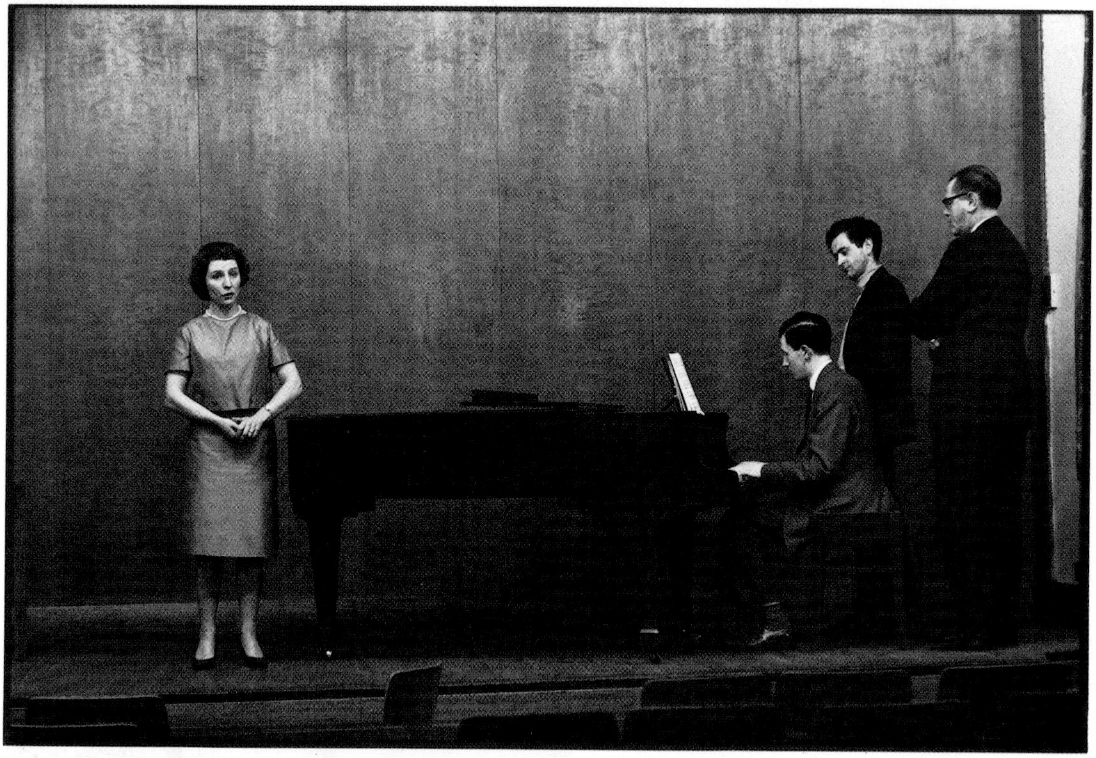

Eve Arnold
Audition, Morley College, London, 1963.

Martine Franck
Colette Magny, 1982.

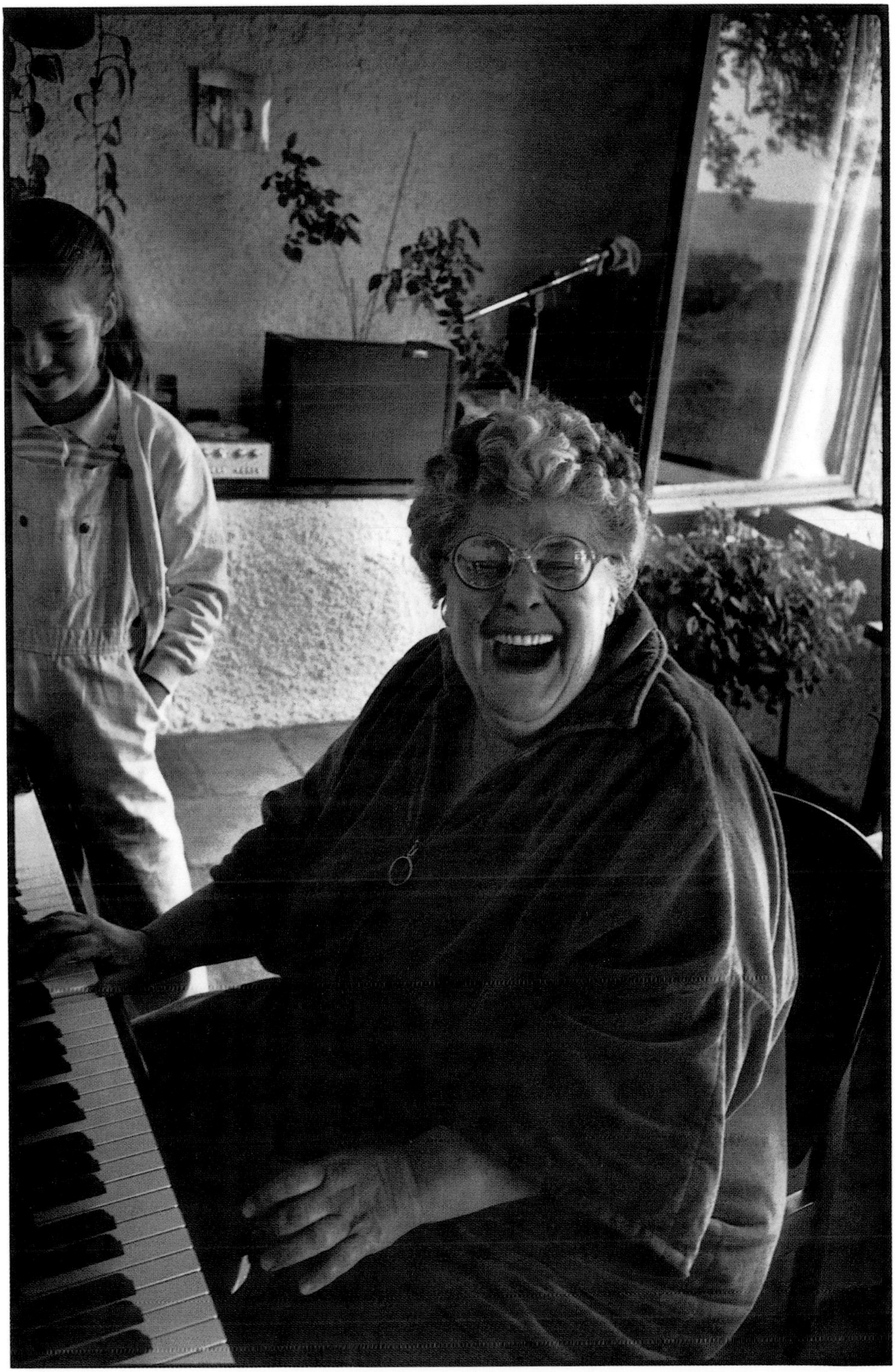

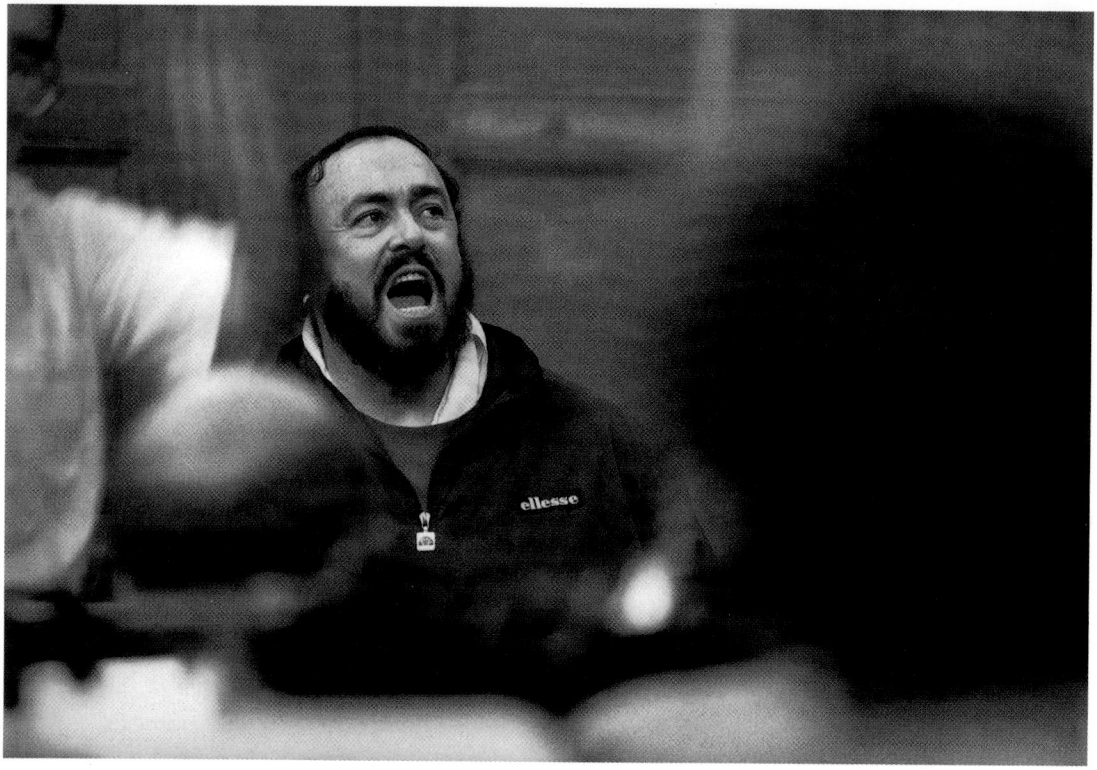

Peter Marlow
Luciano Pavarotti,
1989.

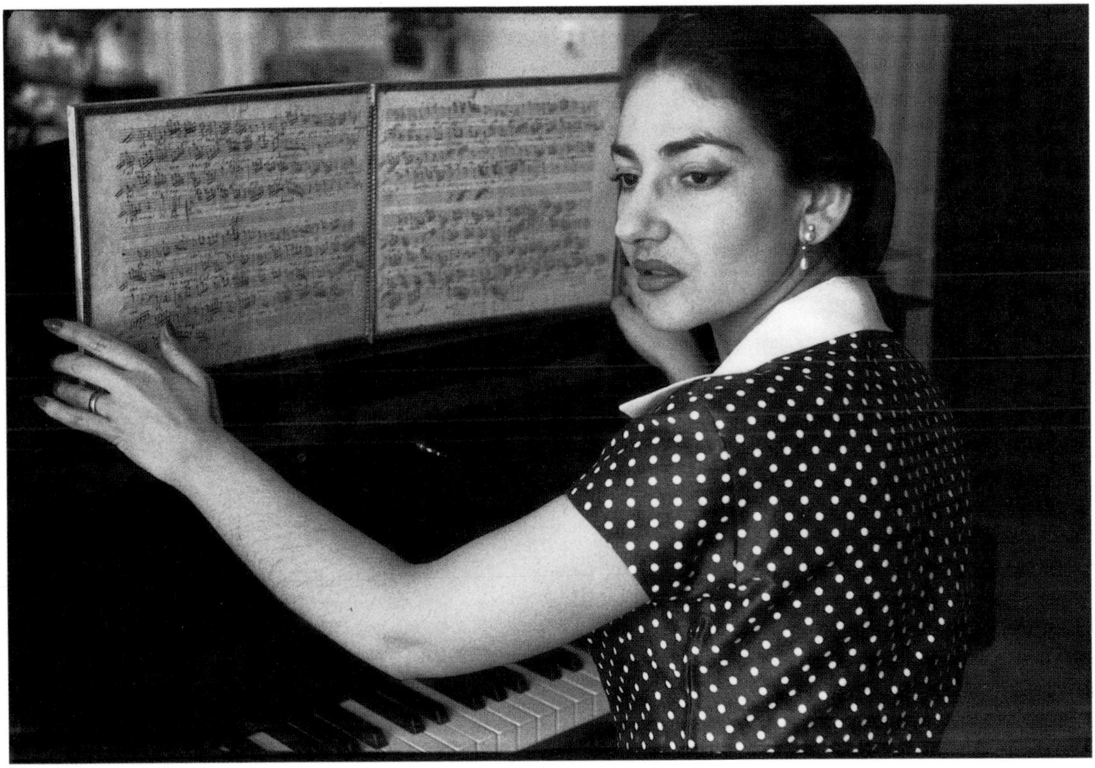

David Seymour
Maria Callas,
1956.

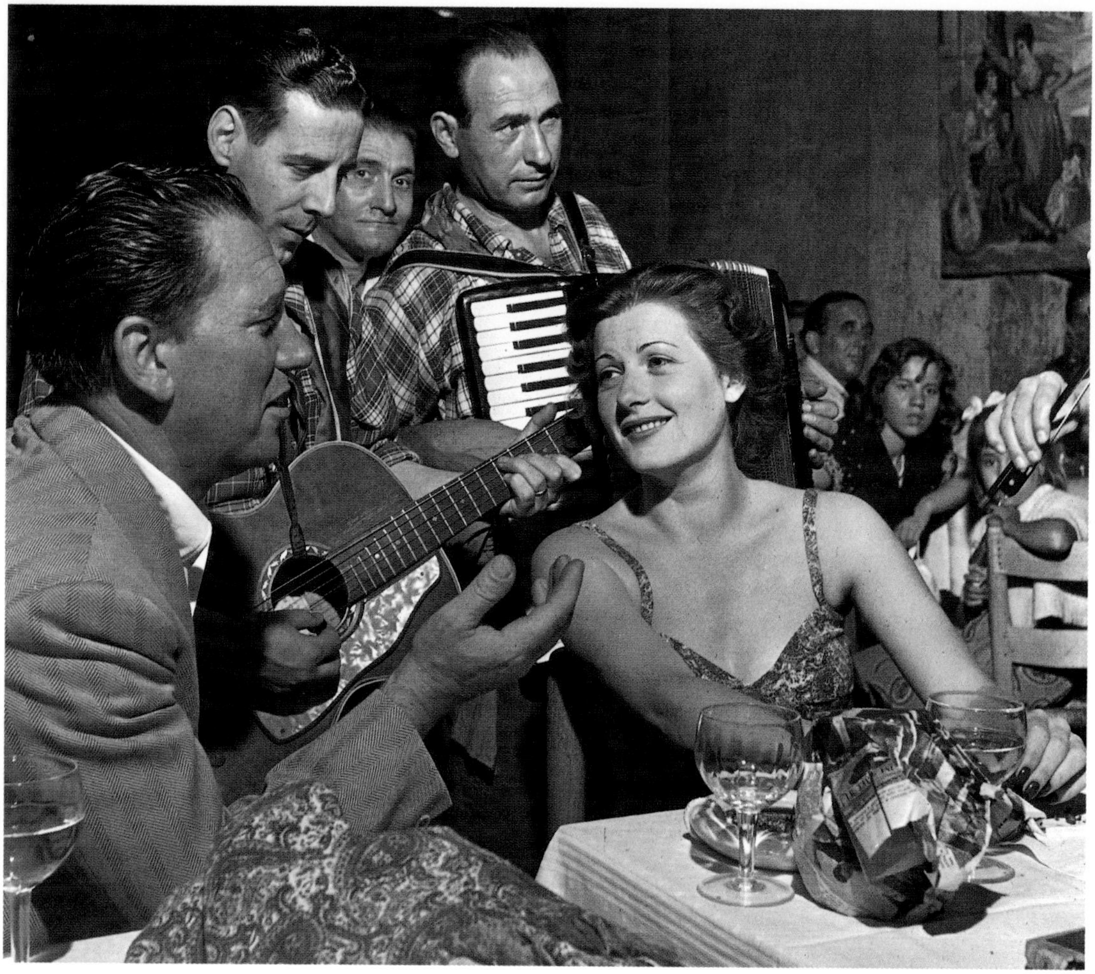

Robert Capa
Rome, 1951.

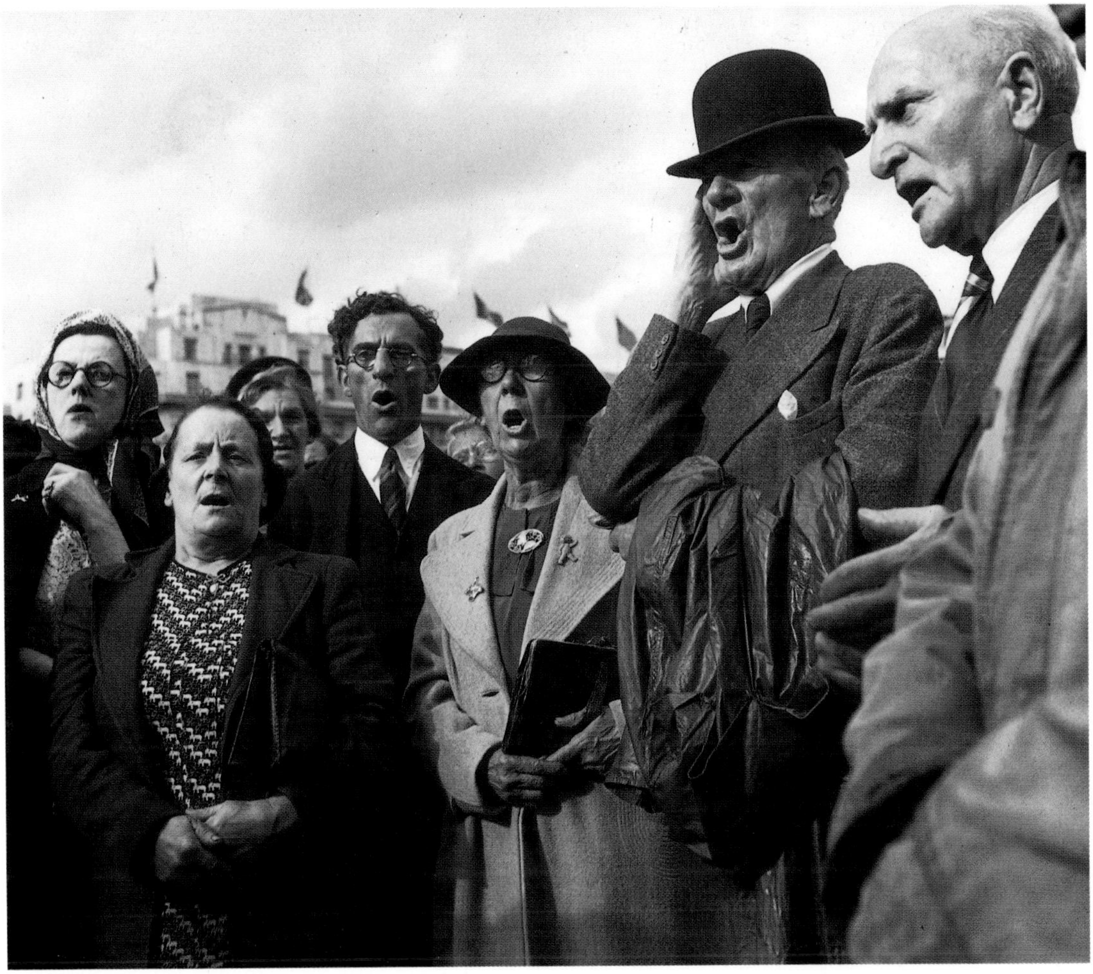

Ernst Haas
Sunday singers in Hyde Park, London, 1947.

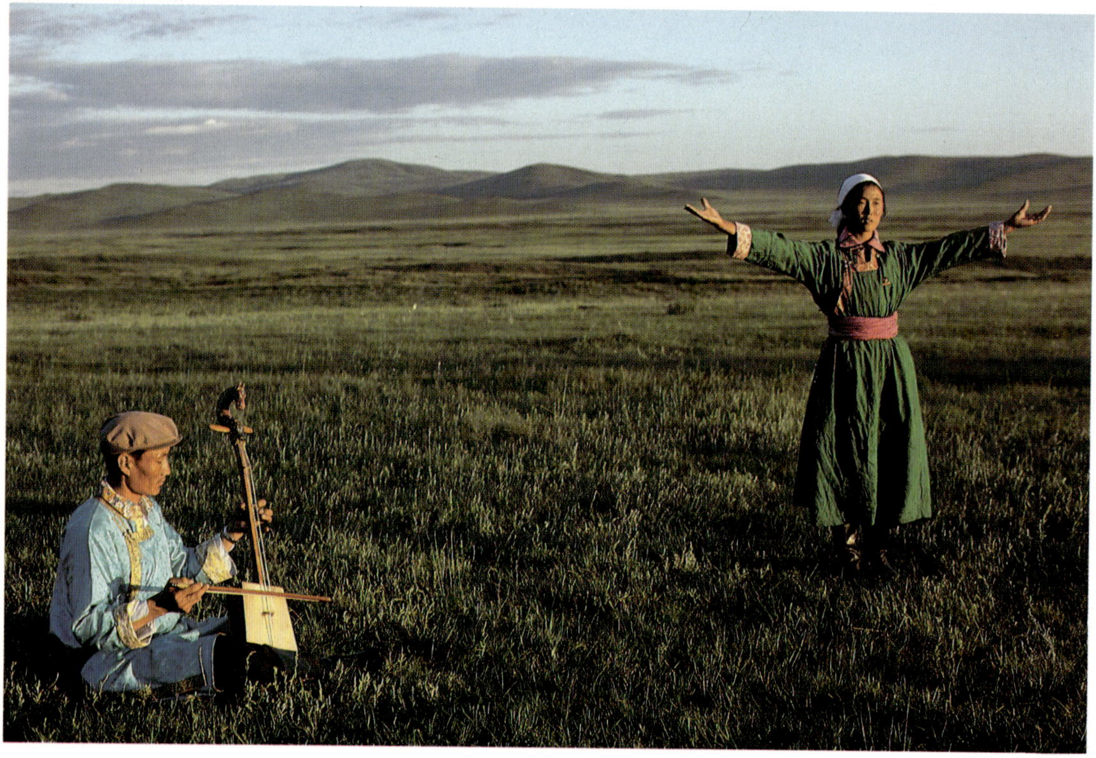

Eve Arnold
Dusk,
Inner Mongolia, 1979.

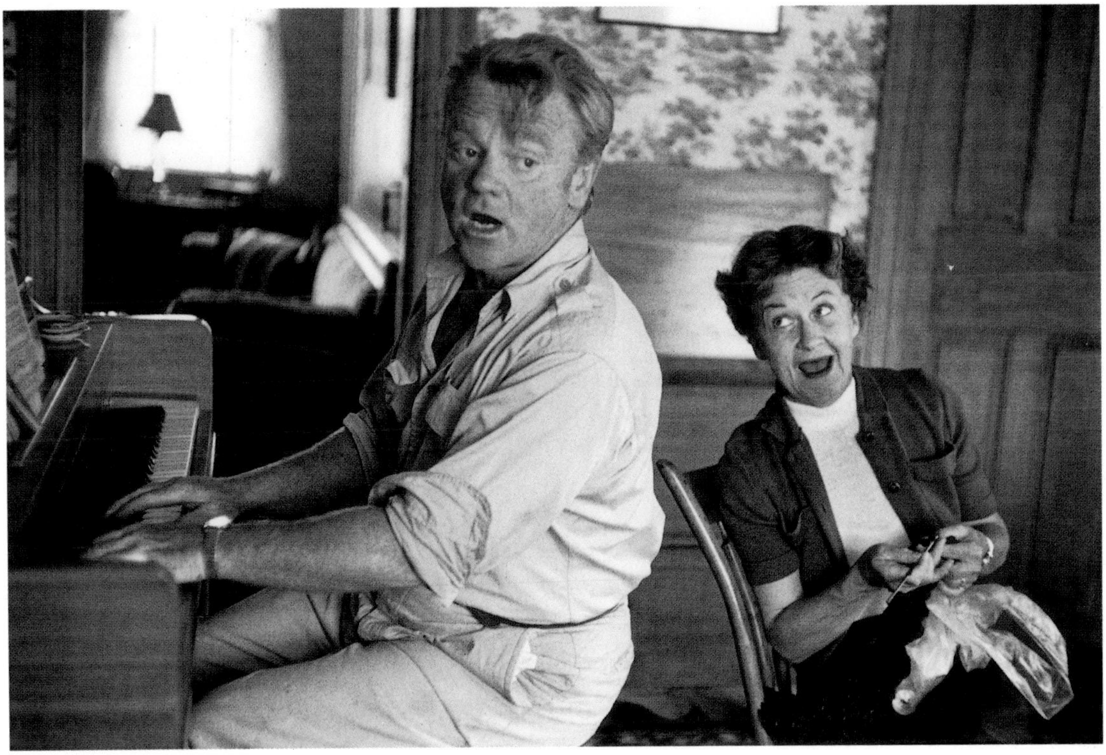

Eve Arnold
James Cagney at home with his wife, 1955.

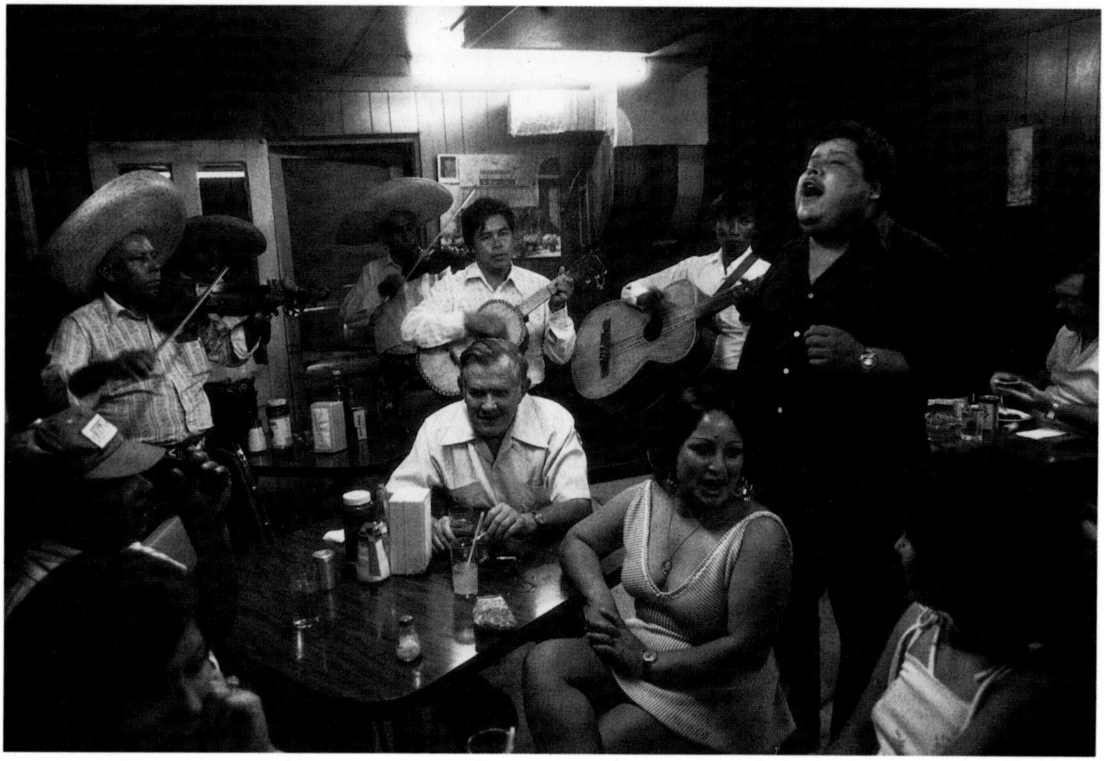

Alex Webb
Bar on the US Frontier, Mexico, 1978.

Ian Berry
Music Festival, Isle of Man, UK, 1979.

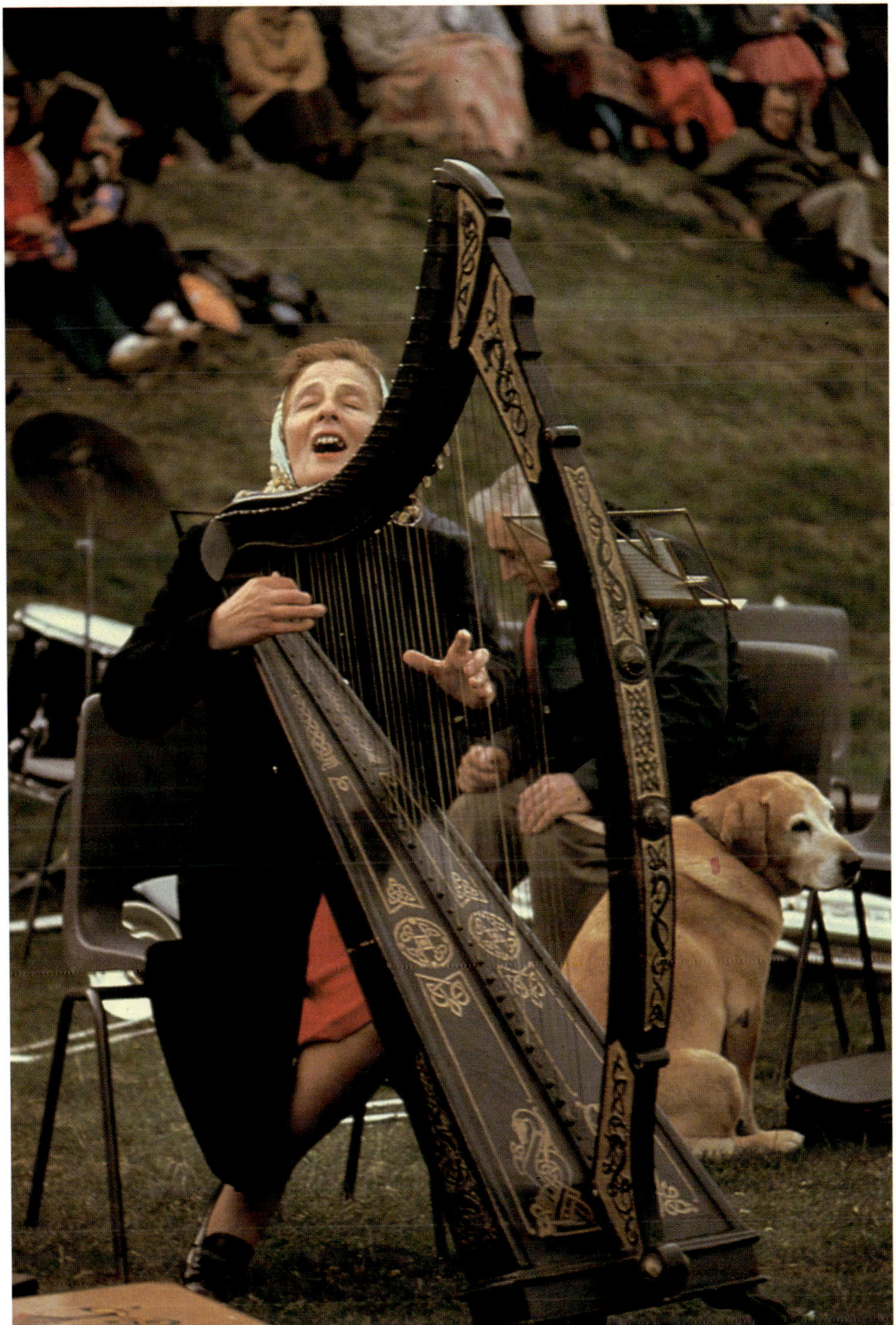

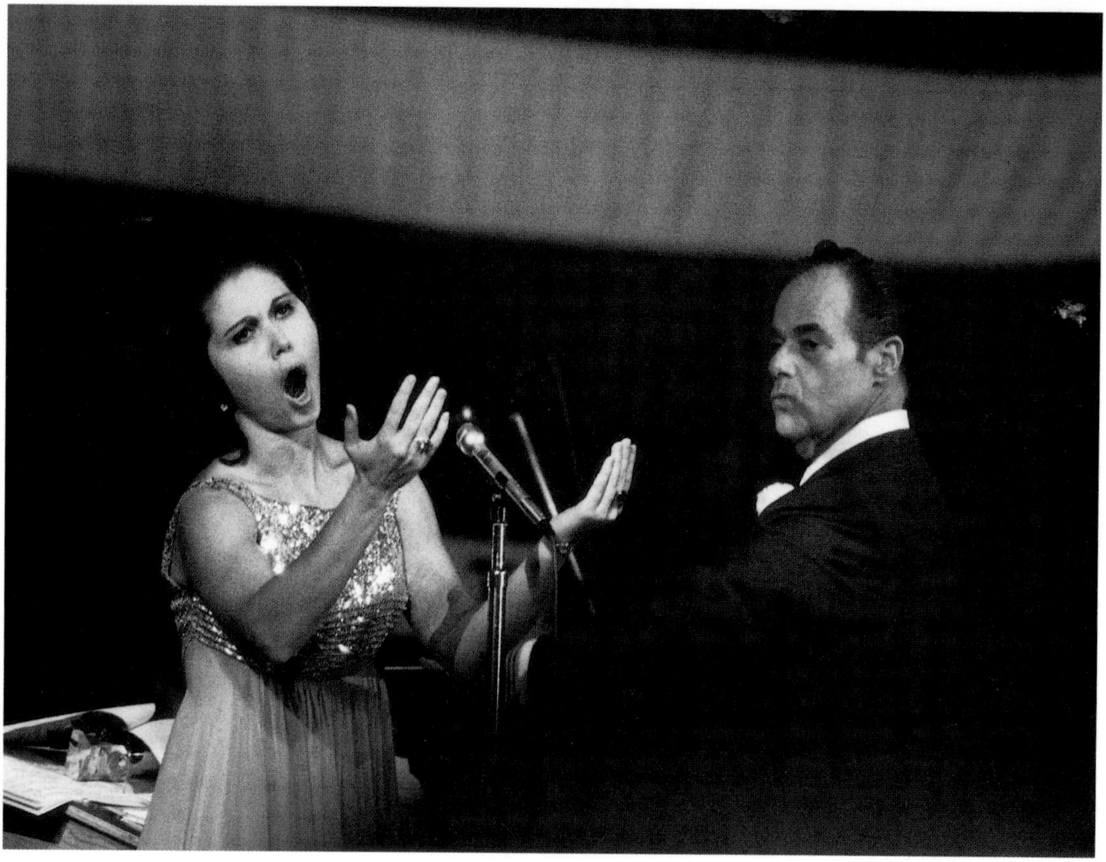

Elliott Erwitt
*Miami Beach,
Florida, 1968.*

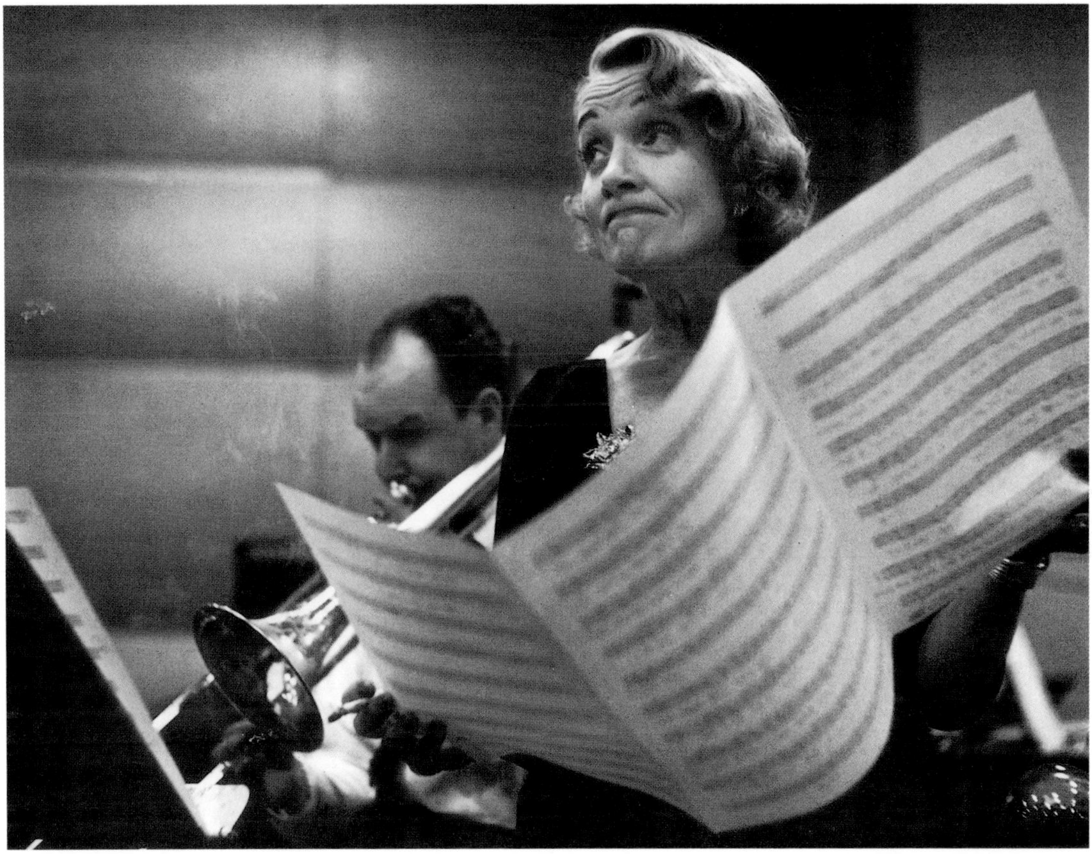

Eve Arnold
Marlene Dietrich, New York Recording Session, 1952.

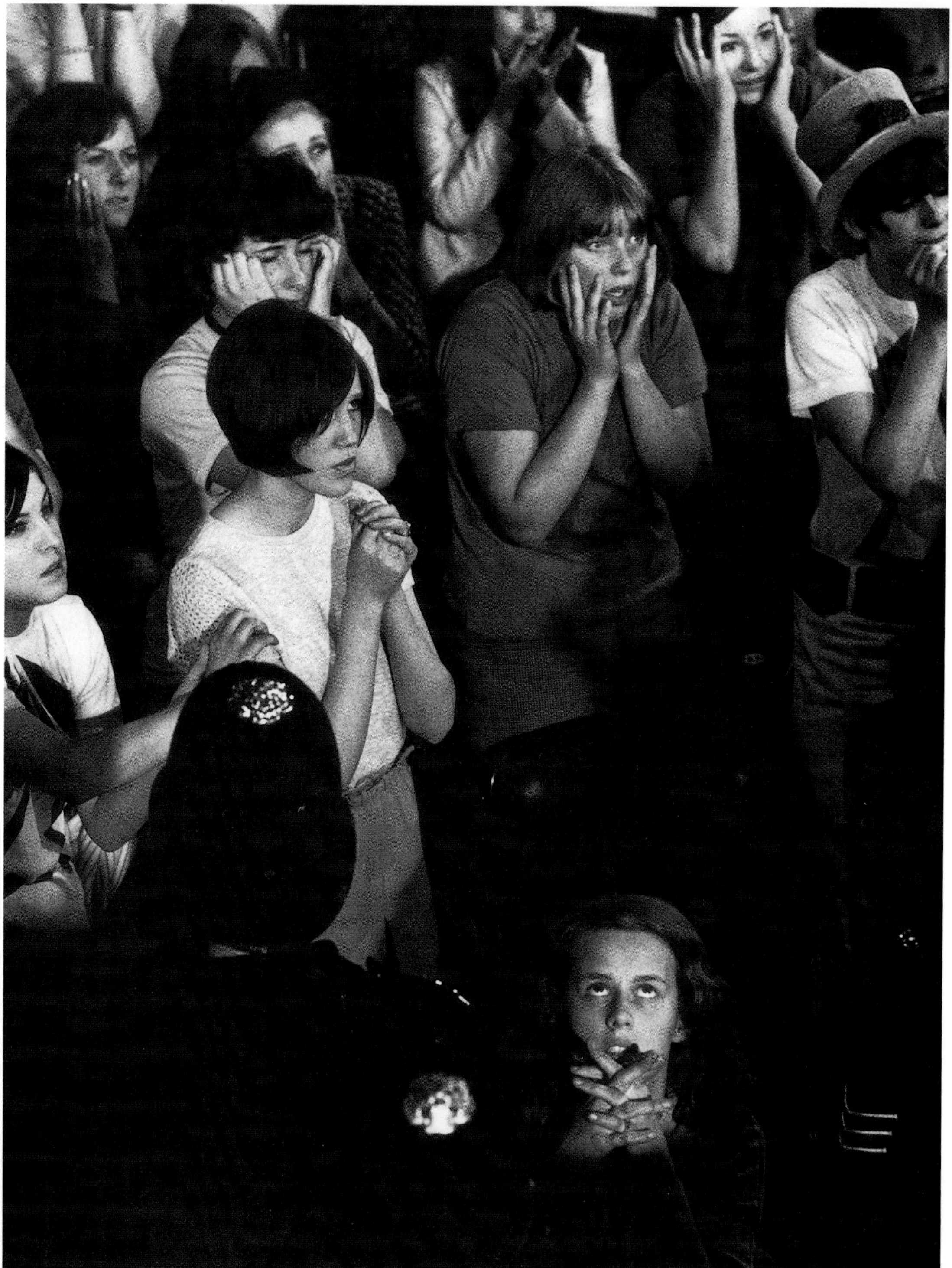

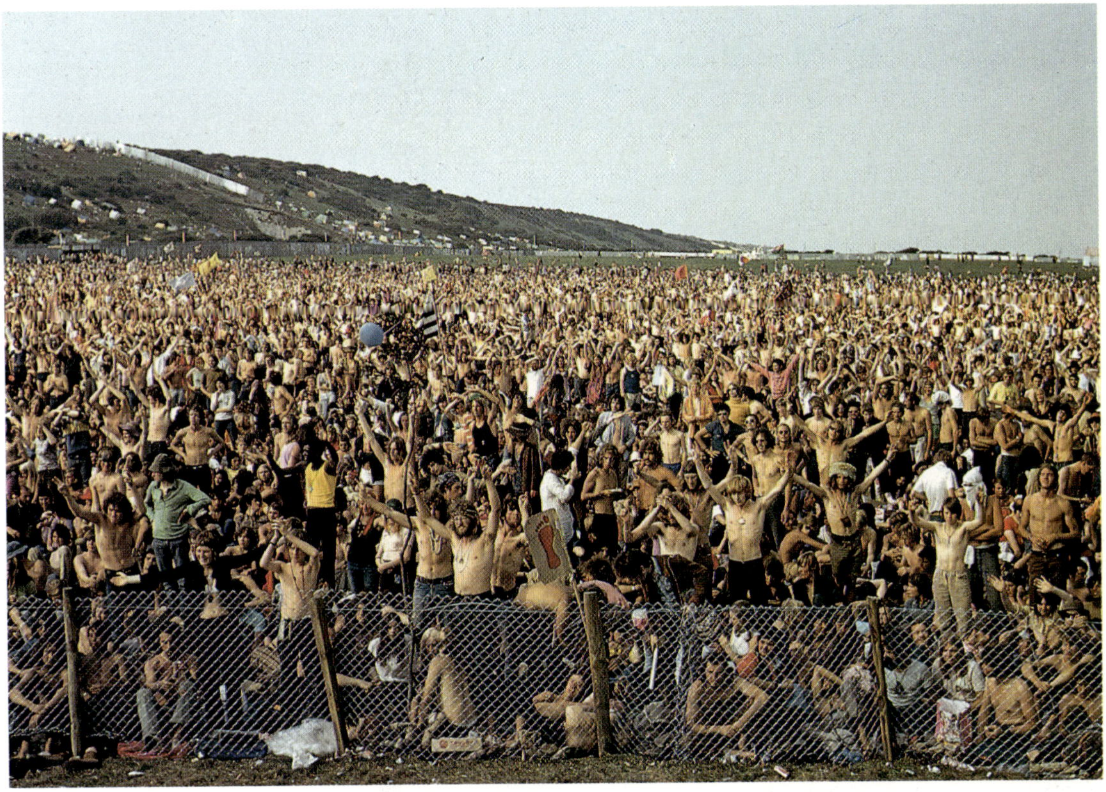

David Hurn
Isle of Wight Rock Festival, UK, 1970.

David Hurn
Beatles concert, 1965.

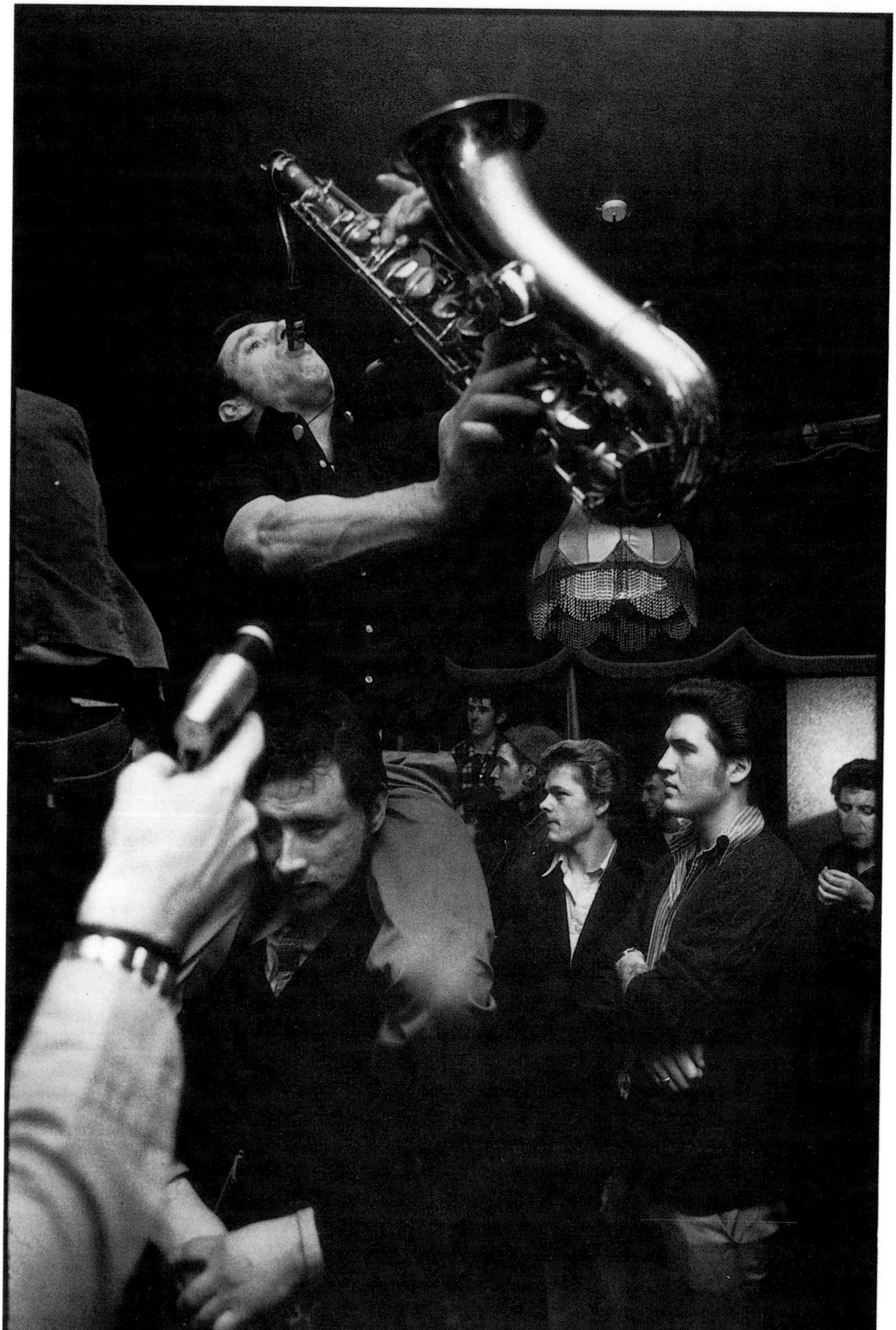

木紫軒

Fleur Chinoise

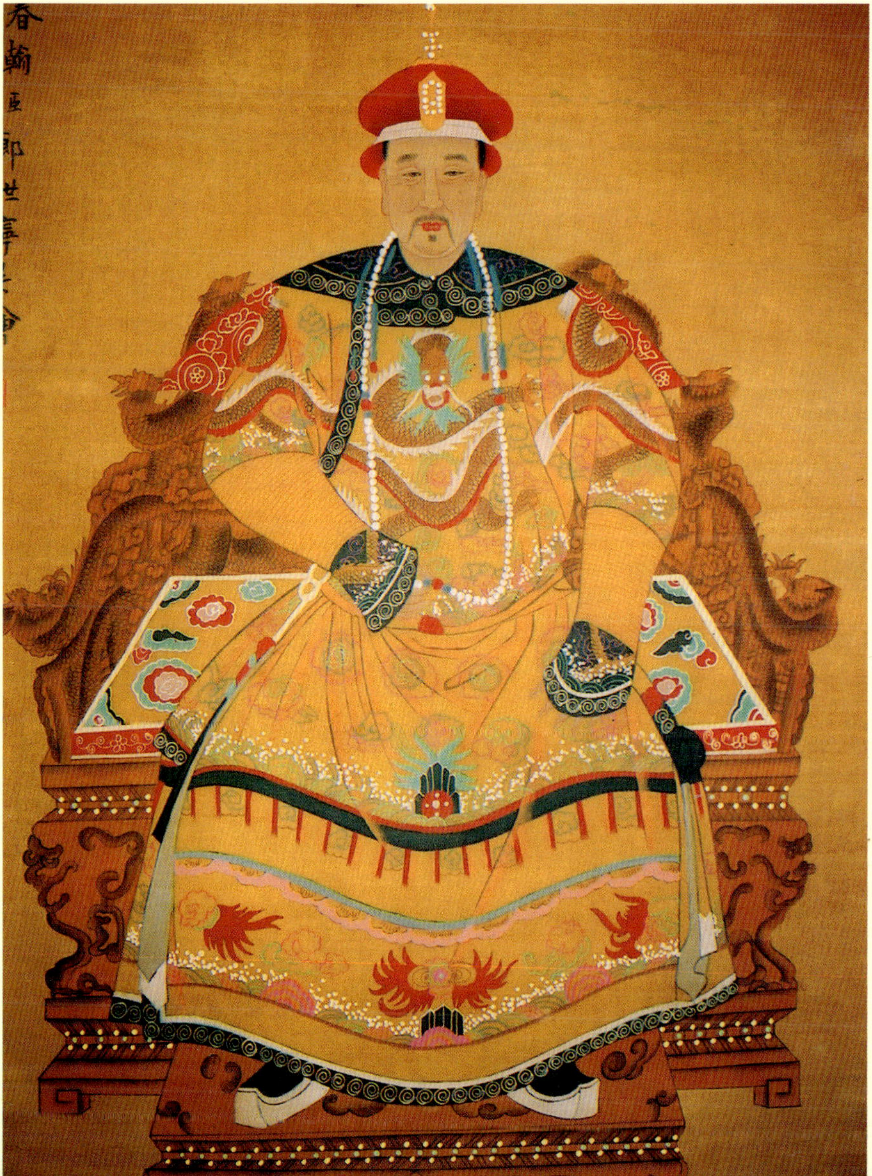

Cabinets

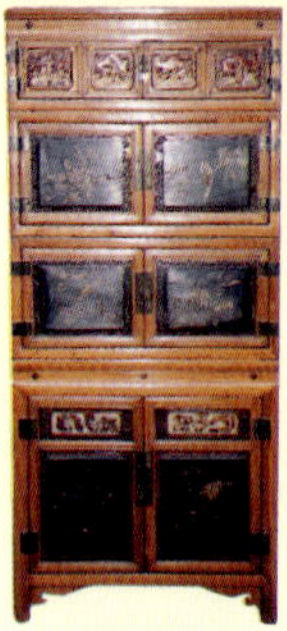

4 pieces Cabinet
四疊柜

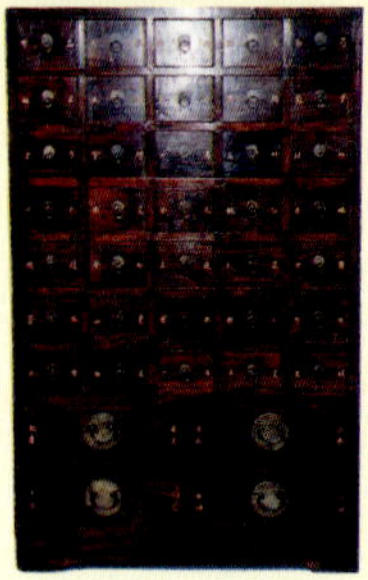

Medicine Cabinet
葯柜

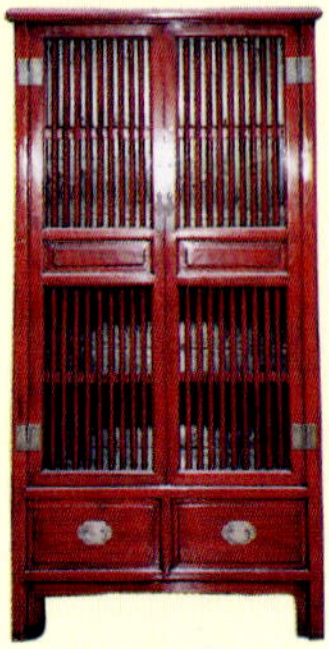

Elm Wood Shelves Cabinet
架格柜

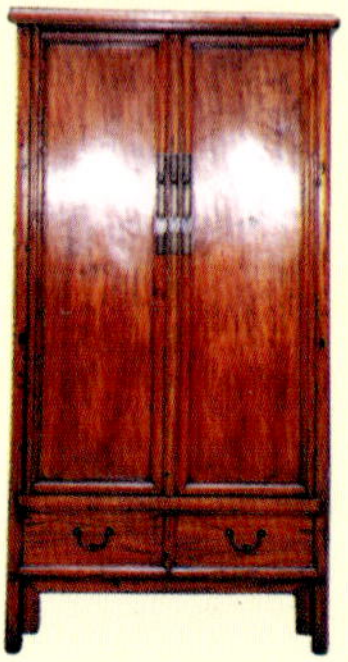

Elm Wood Round
Corner Cabinet
圓角柜

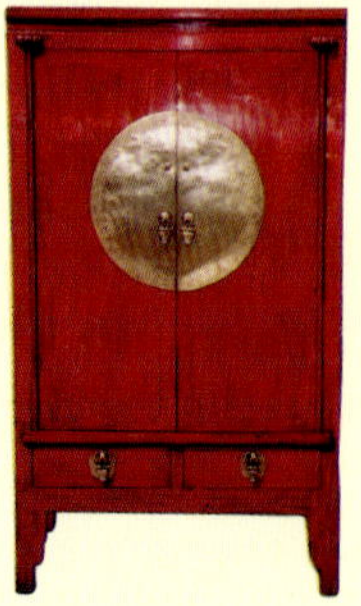

Brass Door Cabinet
銅門柜

Porcelain

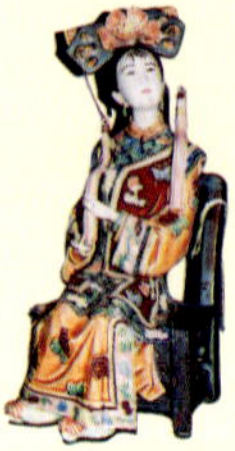

Shek Wan Figurine
10″ High

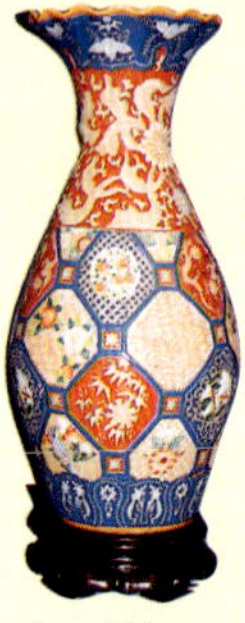

Imari Vase
14″ High

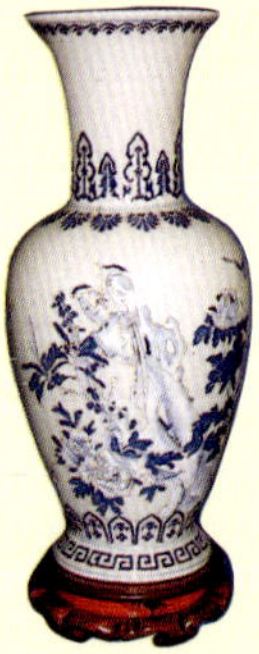

Blue & White Vase
14″ High

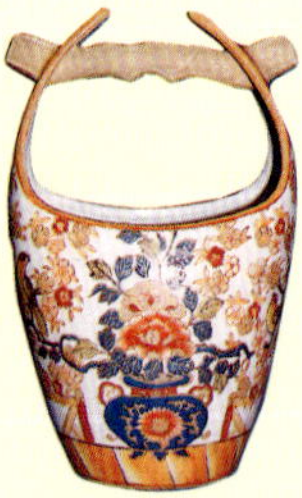

Water Bucket Shape Vase
12″ High

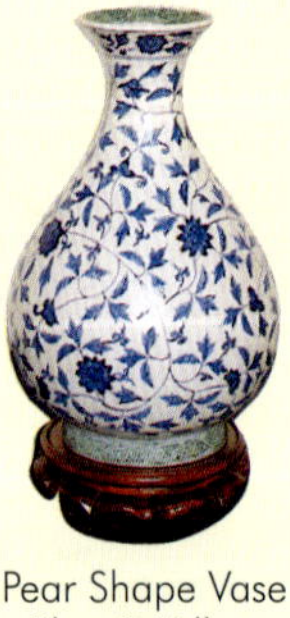

Pear Shape Vase
Blue & Yellow
14″ High

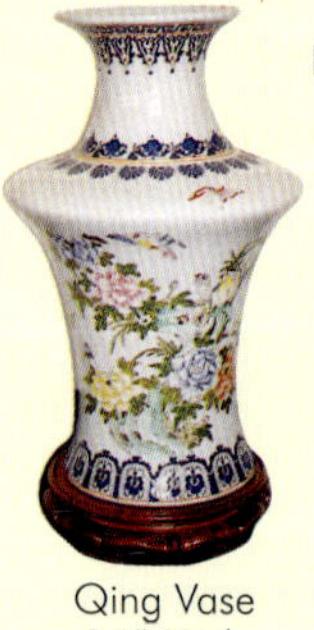

Qing Vase
14″ High

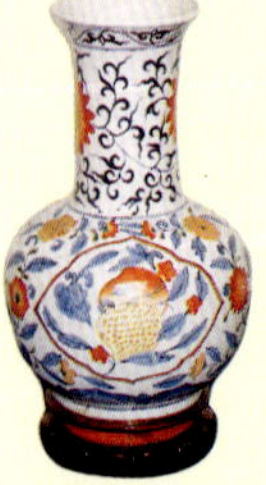

Bell Shape Vase
12″ High

Tables & Chairs

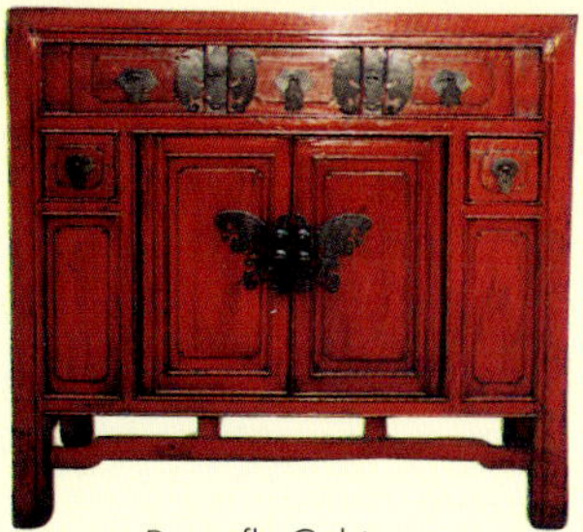

Butterfly Cabinet
蝴蝶柜

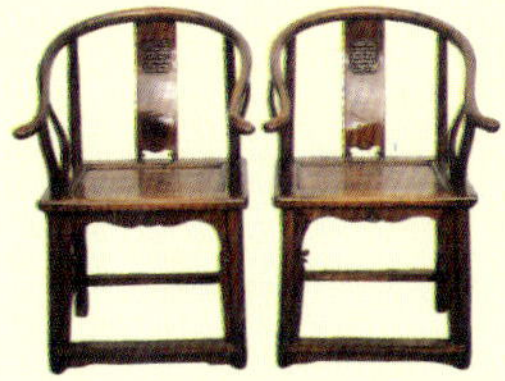

Armchair with Curved Rest
圓椅

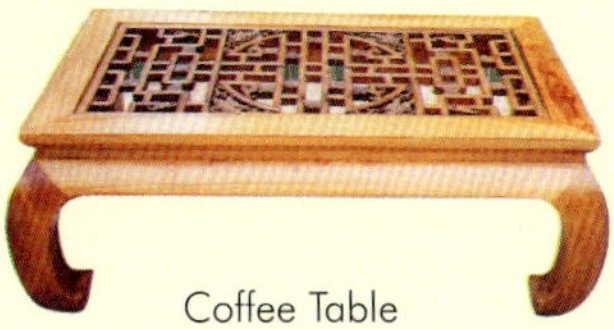

Coffee Table
咖啡檯

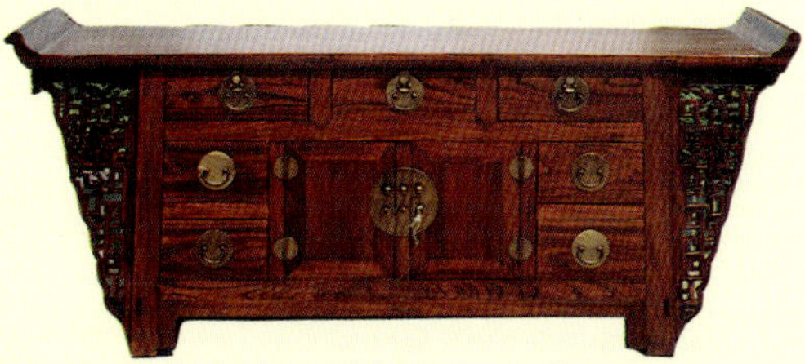

Elm Wood 7 Drawer Coffer
七聯柜

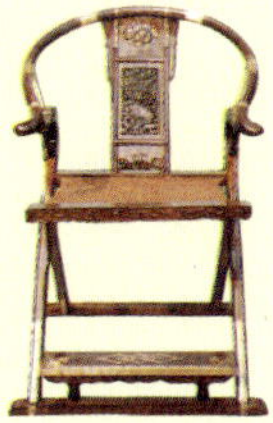

Folding Armchair
圓背交椅

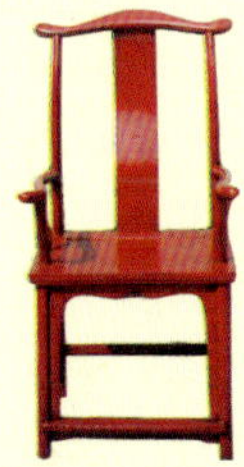

Official Hat Armchair
官帽椅

Artefacts & Flowers

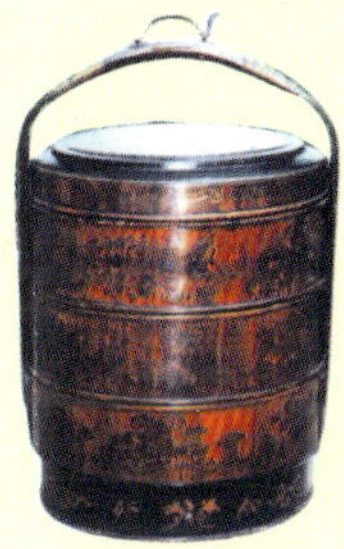

Wedding Basket
禮盒

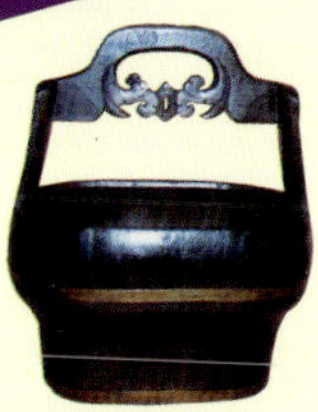

Water Bucket
水桶

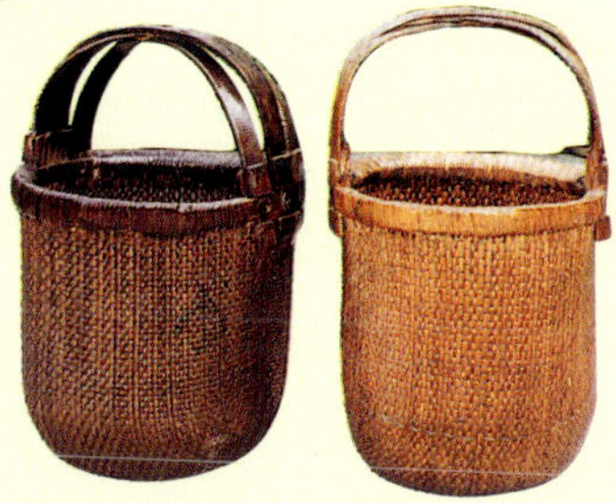

Willow Basket
柳籃

Tea Bucket
茶桶

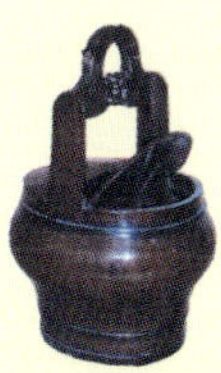

Food Carrier
提盒

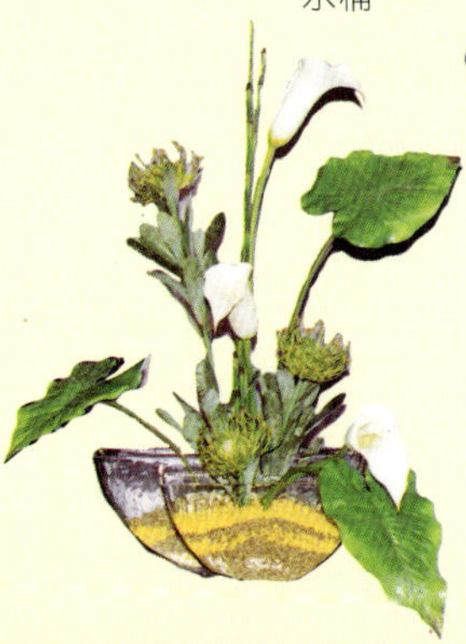

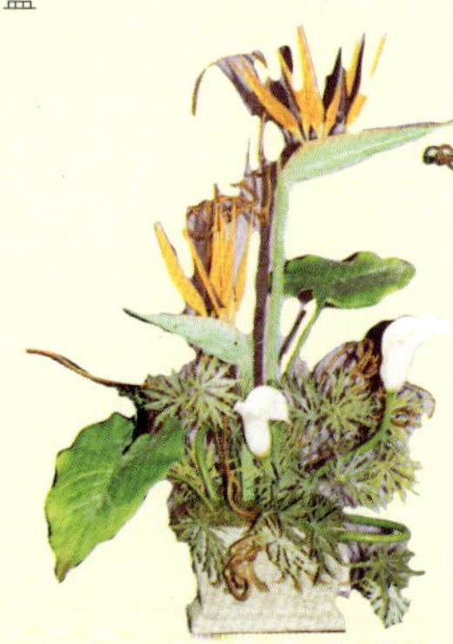

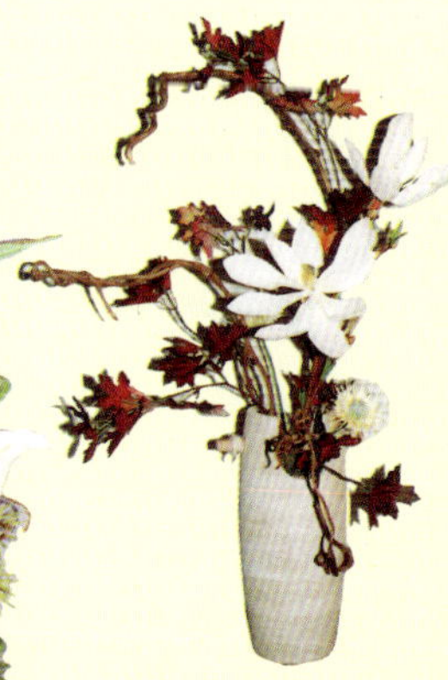

About Fleur Chinoise

Founded in June 1999 by Susanna & Peter Bassett, Fleur Chinsoise specialises in the sale of personally sourced Chinese furniture, artefacts and porcelain, imported directly from China.

Susanna, a Hong Kong born Chinese lady with a very strong knowledge of Period Chinese furniture and the many known Chinese artefacts, has the ability to create and design any layout to your desire or taste. Susanna can also add that special touch with her love for flower arranging and can transform any environment into one that is pleasing to the eye. A certificated Constance Spry student, Susanna can add floral arrangements with that "Oriental Touch", to an individual piece of furniture or room.

Peter, who lived and worked in Hong Kong for over twenty years, has an excellent knowledge of Chinese culture, the way of life in the Far East and the many Chinese items that are on display in their shop and in their extensive store.

The furniture, imported from China, is sourced and refurbished to Susanna's or the client's own individual taste and is dated in some cases to over 100 years old. All pieces are original and unique. The furniture ranges from Classic Altar Tables to Linen Cabinets, Kitchen Cabinets, Chairs, Benches, Beds and Screens.

The porcelain, which ranges from Vases, Lamp Stands, Charger Plates and Ornamental features are reproductions from the Tang, Ming and Qing Dynasties, with an assortment of designs and colours, which are specific to the reigning Emperors of that particular period.

With a miscellaneous assortment of Chinese artefacts ranging from Chinese Figurines to Terracotta Warriors, Embroidered Silk Cloth to Leather Opium Boxes and Trunks, Fleur Chinoise has something for you.

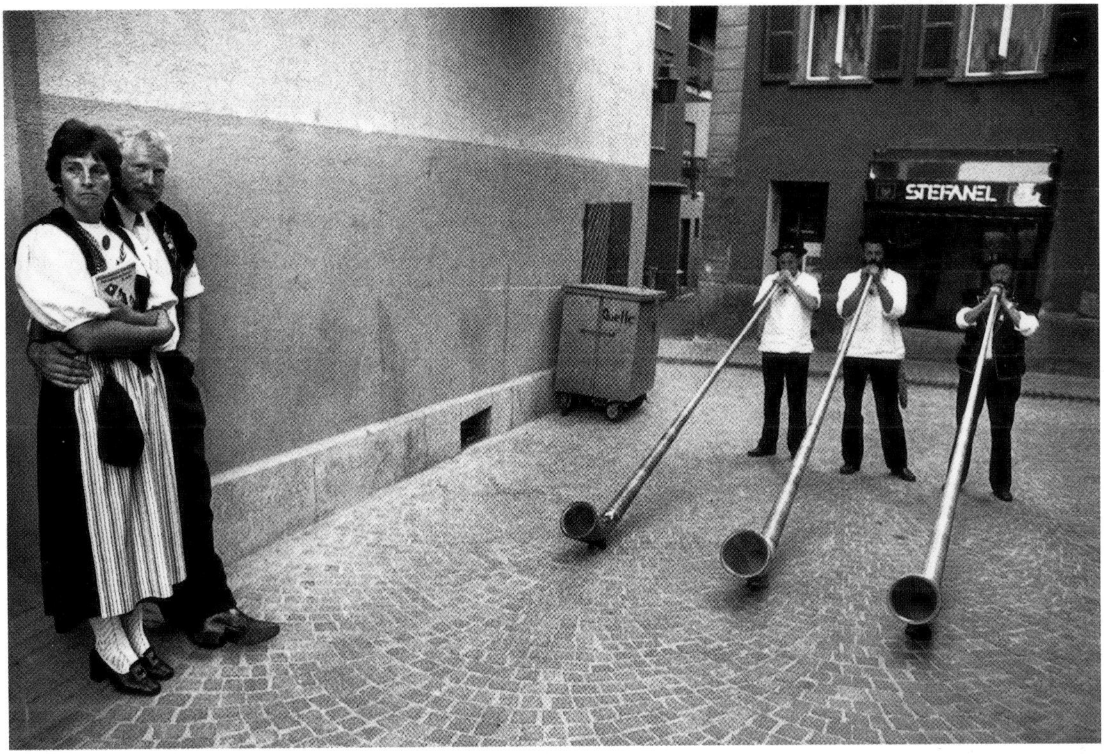

Sebastiao Salgado
Alpine horn players at a yodelling festival, Brig, Switzerland, 1987.

Chris Steele-Perkins
'The Flying Saucers', UK, 1976.

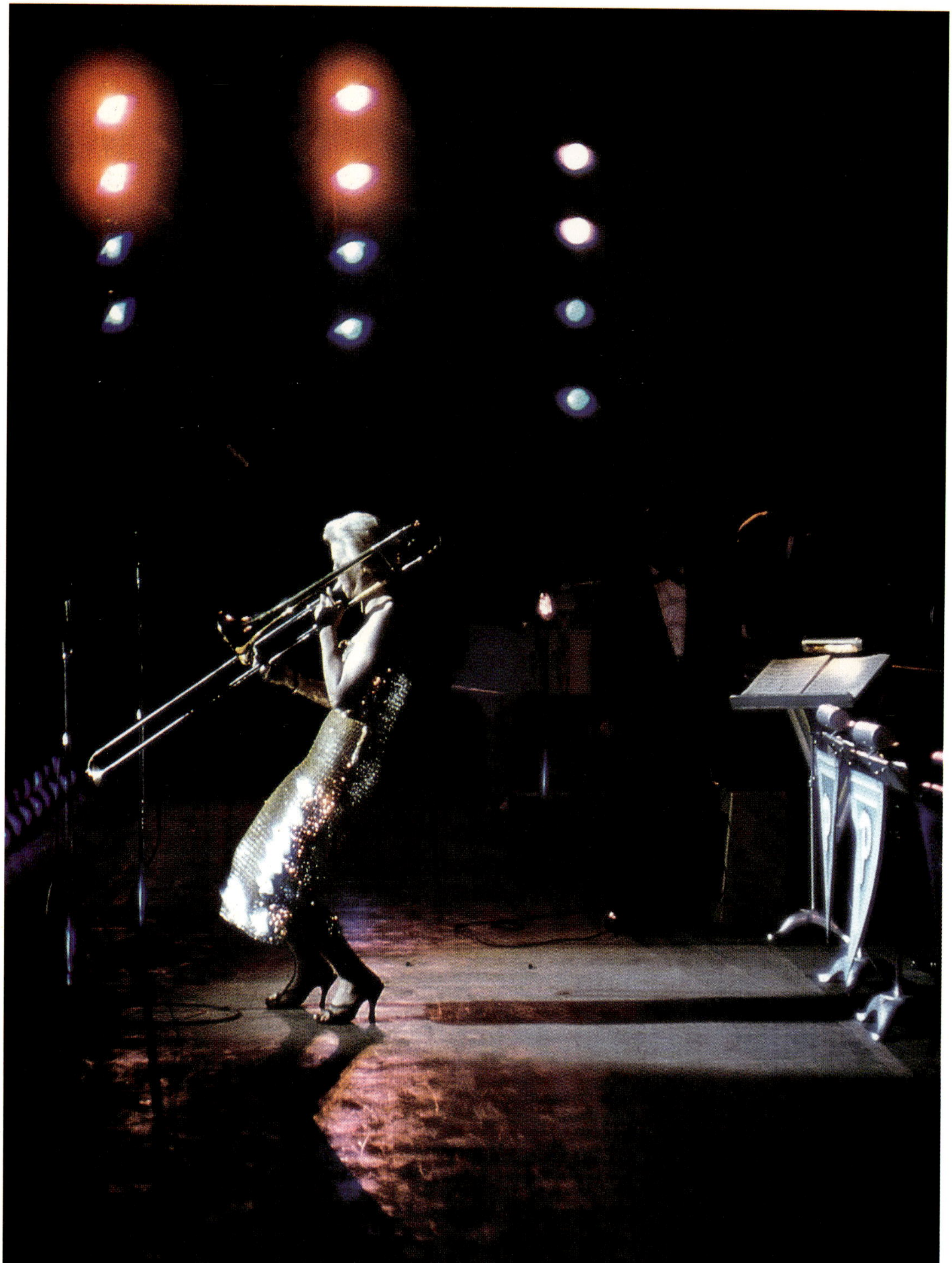

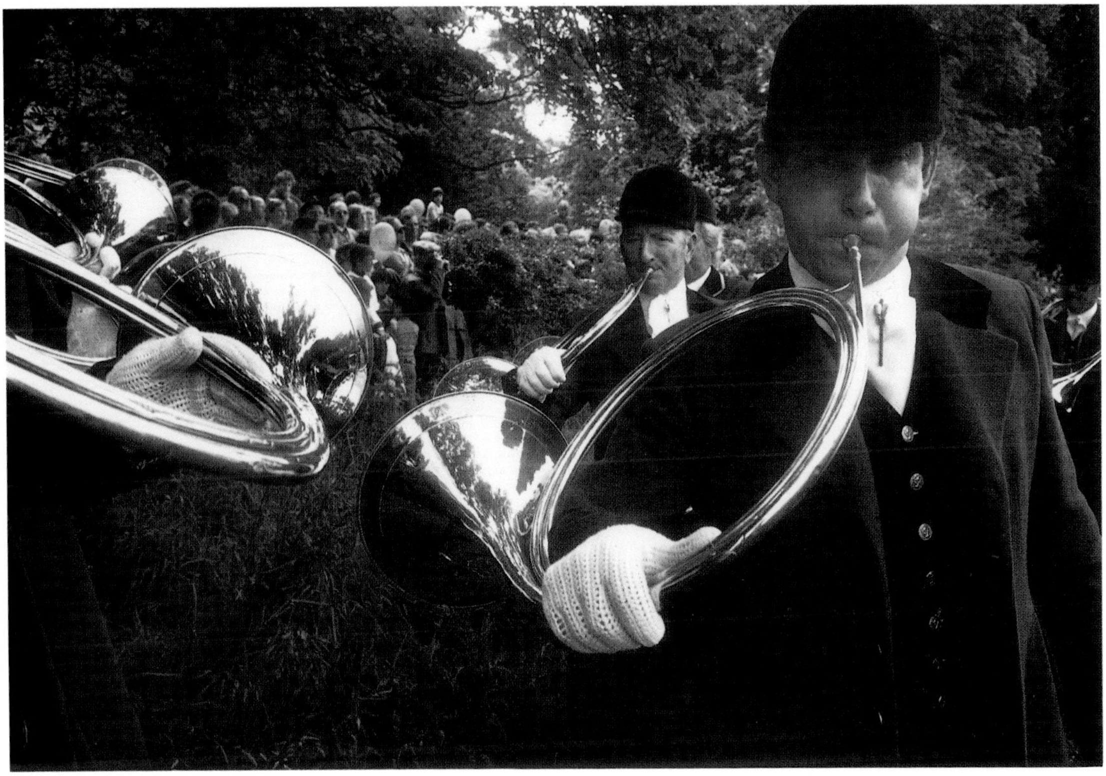

Sebastiao Salgado
Hunting corps, Balleroy, France, 1980.

Eve Arnold
Lillian Briggs, Brooklyn, New York, 1977.

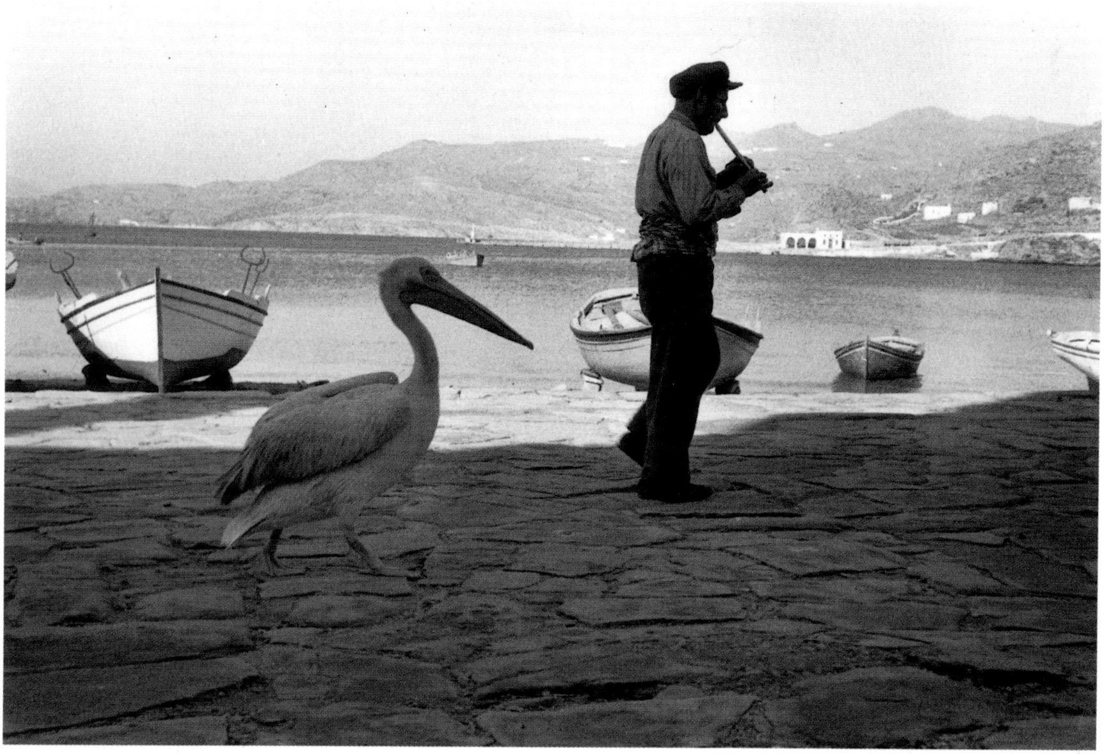

René Burri
Mykonos, Greece, 1957.

Dennis Stock
Charlie Parker, Mercury Recording Studios, USA.

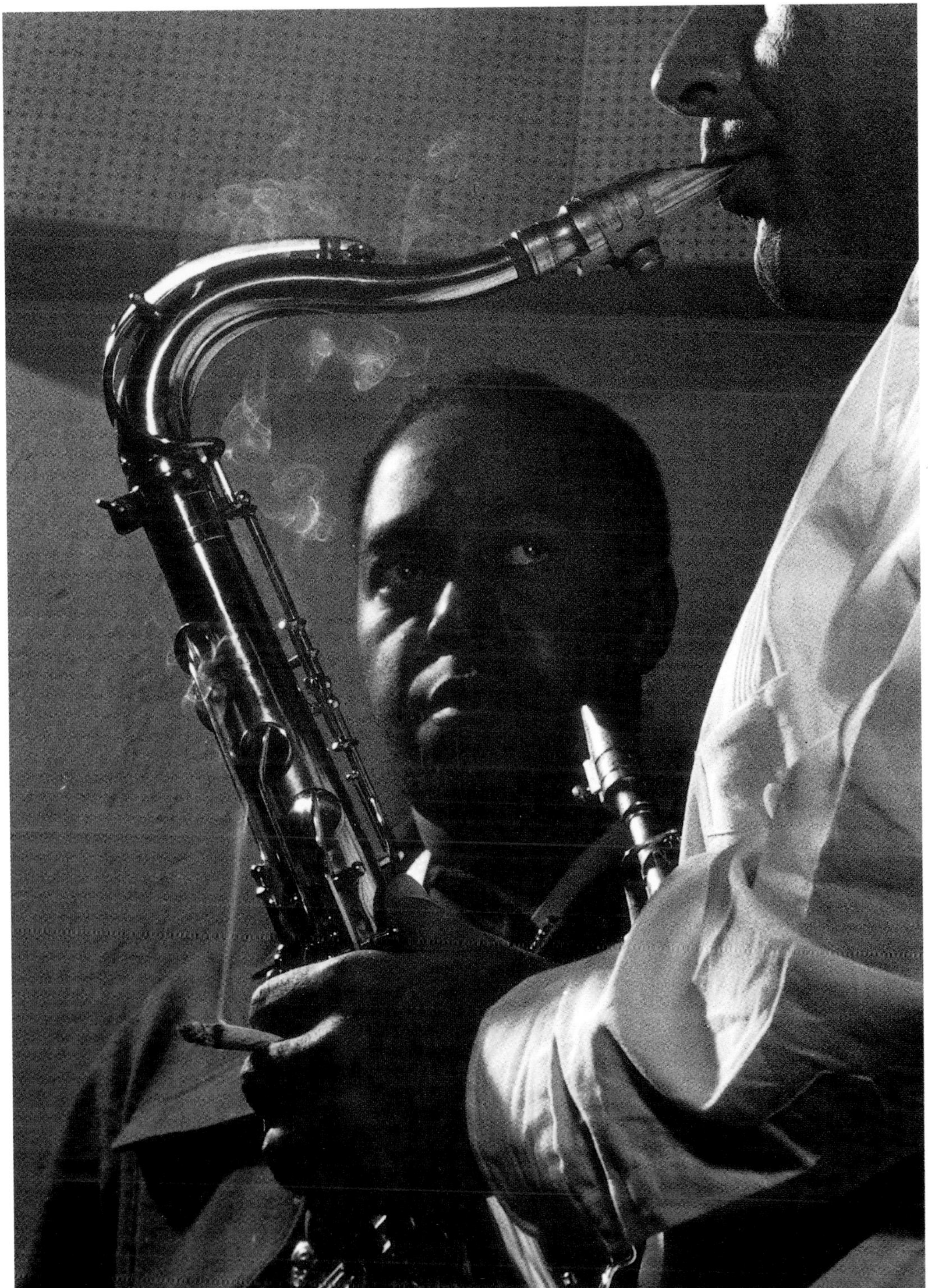

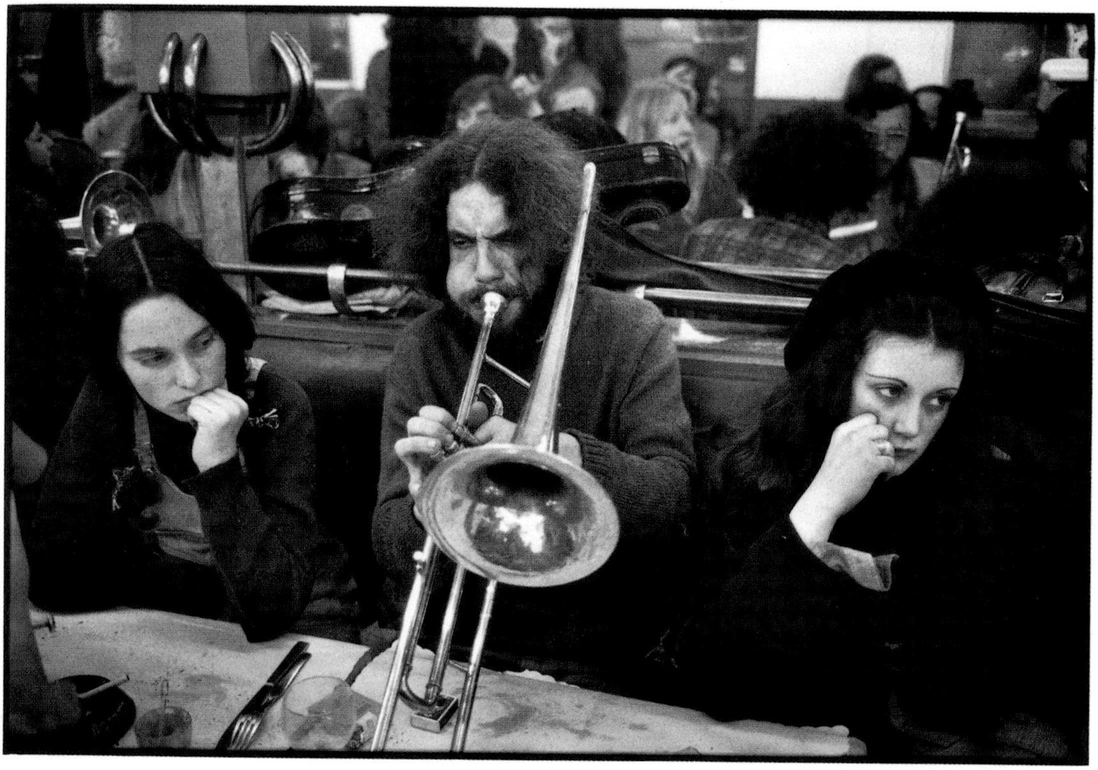

Guy Le Querrec
Cafe 'La Biere',
Paris.

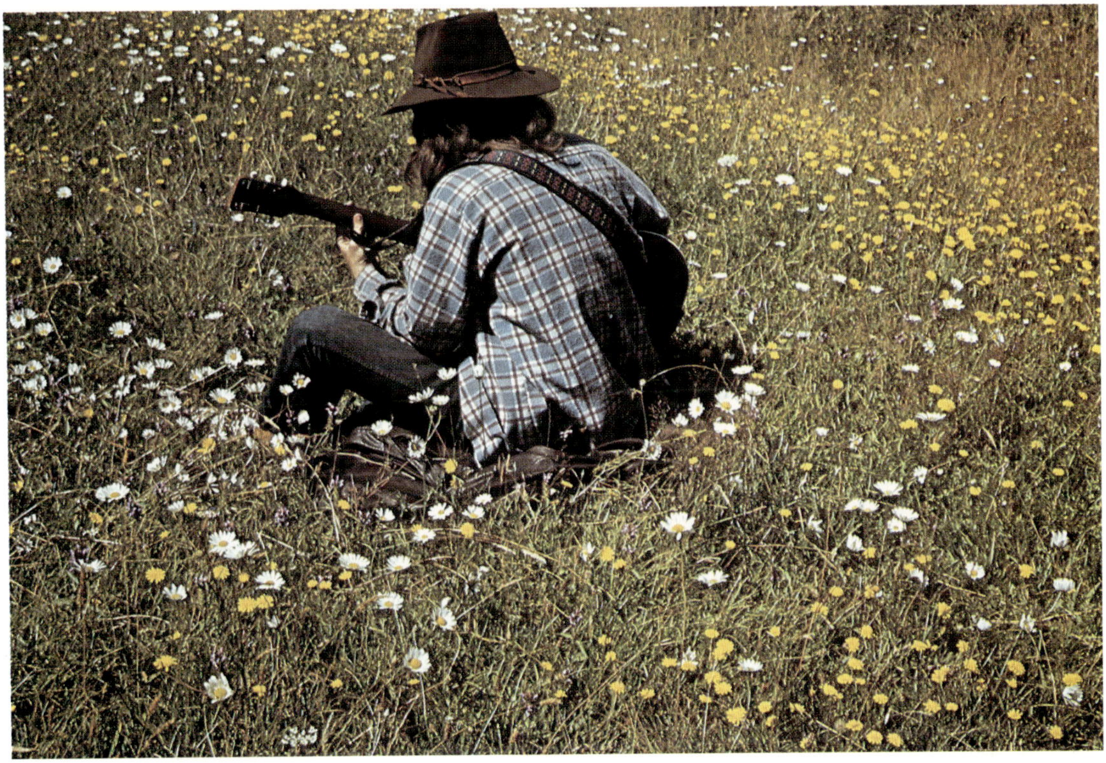

Dennis Stock
Alaska, 1975.

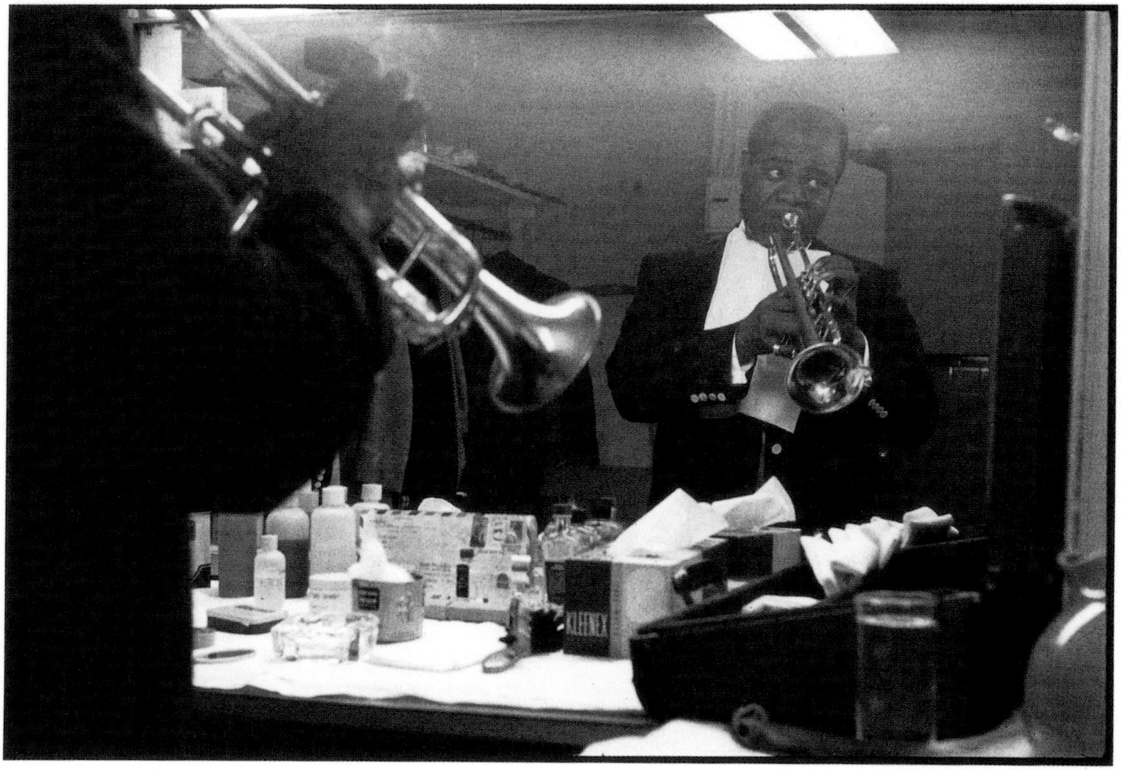

Dennis Stock
Louis Armstrong, 1958.

Paul Fusco
Untitled, 1989.

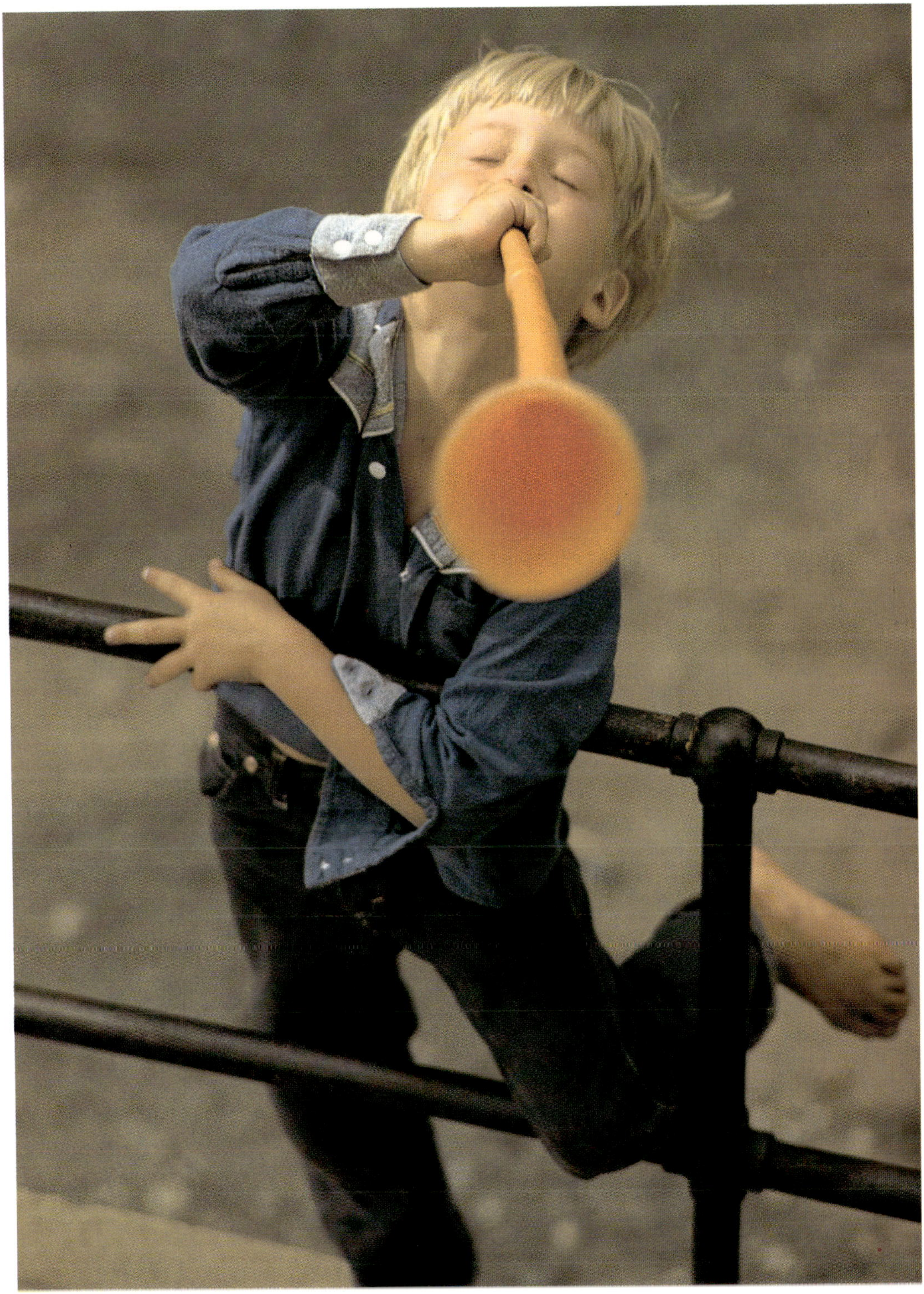

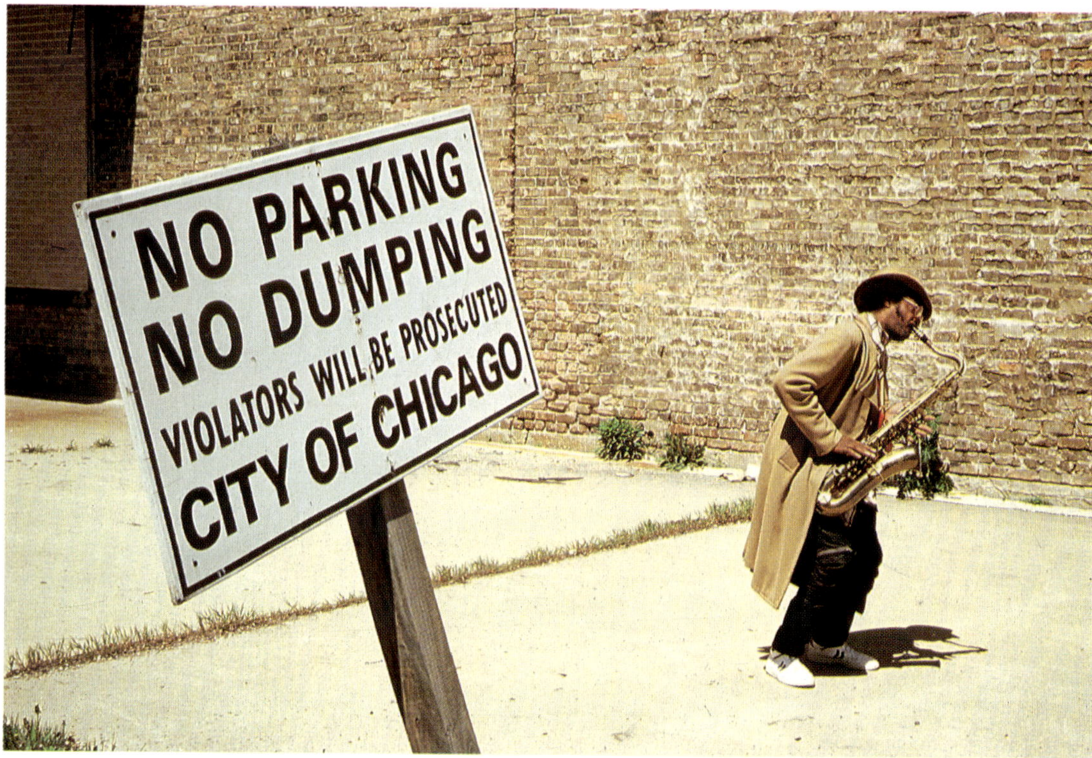

Leonard Freed
Cabrini Green, Busker, Chicago, 1987.

Burt Glinn
50s entertainers, USA.

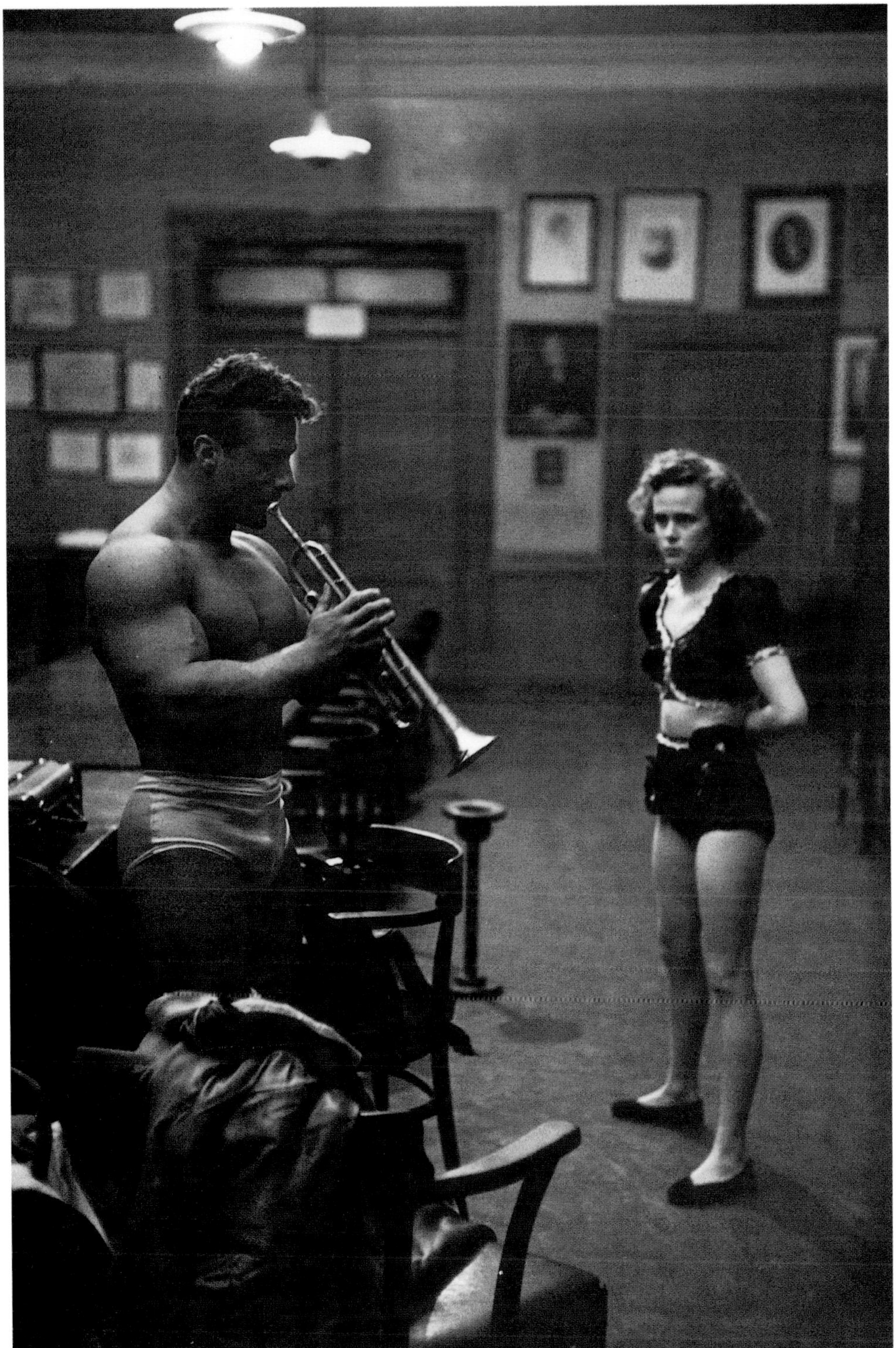

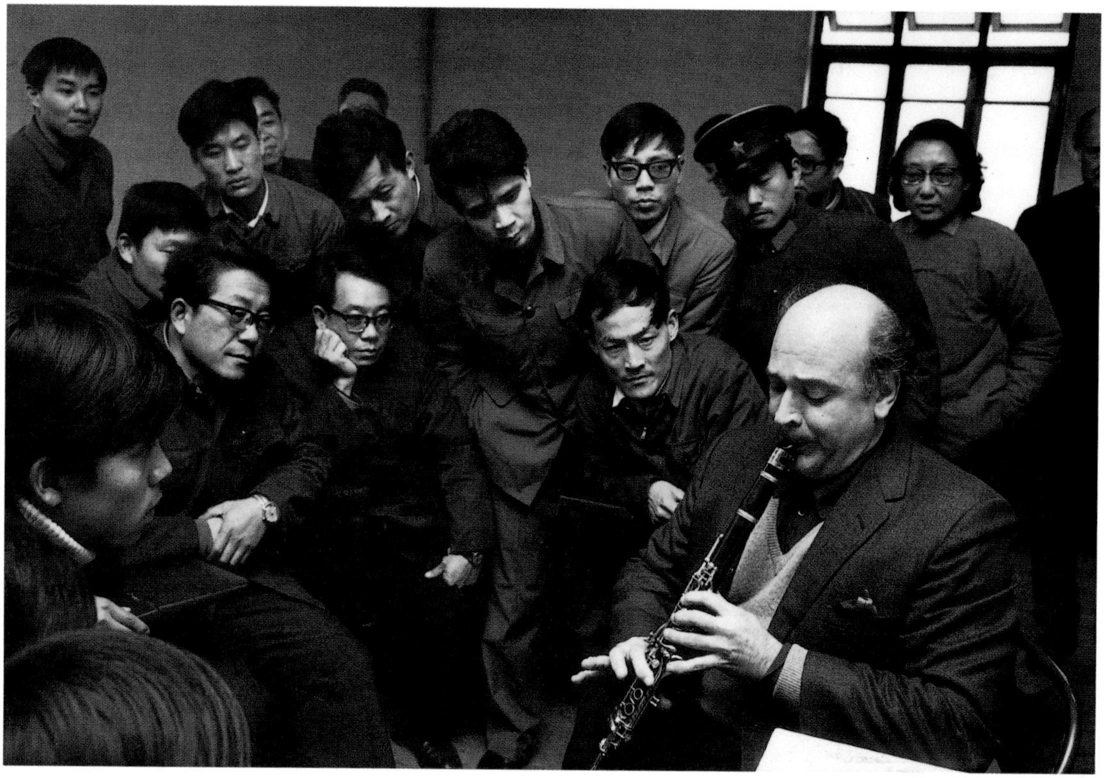

Costa Manos
Boston Symphony Orchestra in China, 1979.

Sebastiao Salgado
Unos Indians, Lake Titicaca, Peru, 1977.

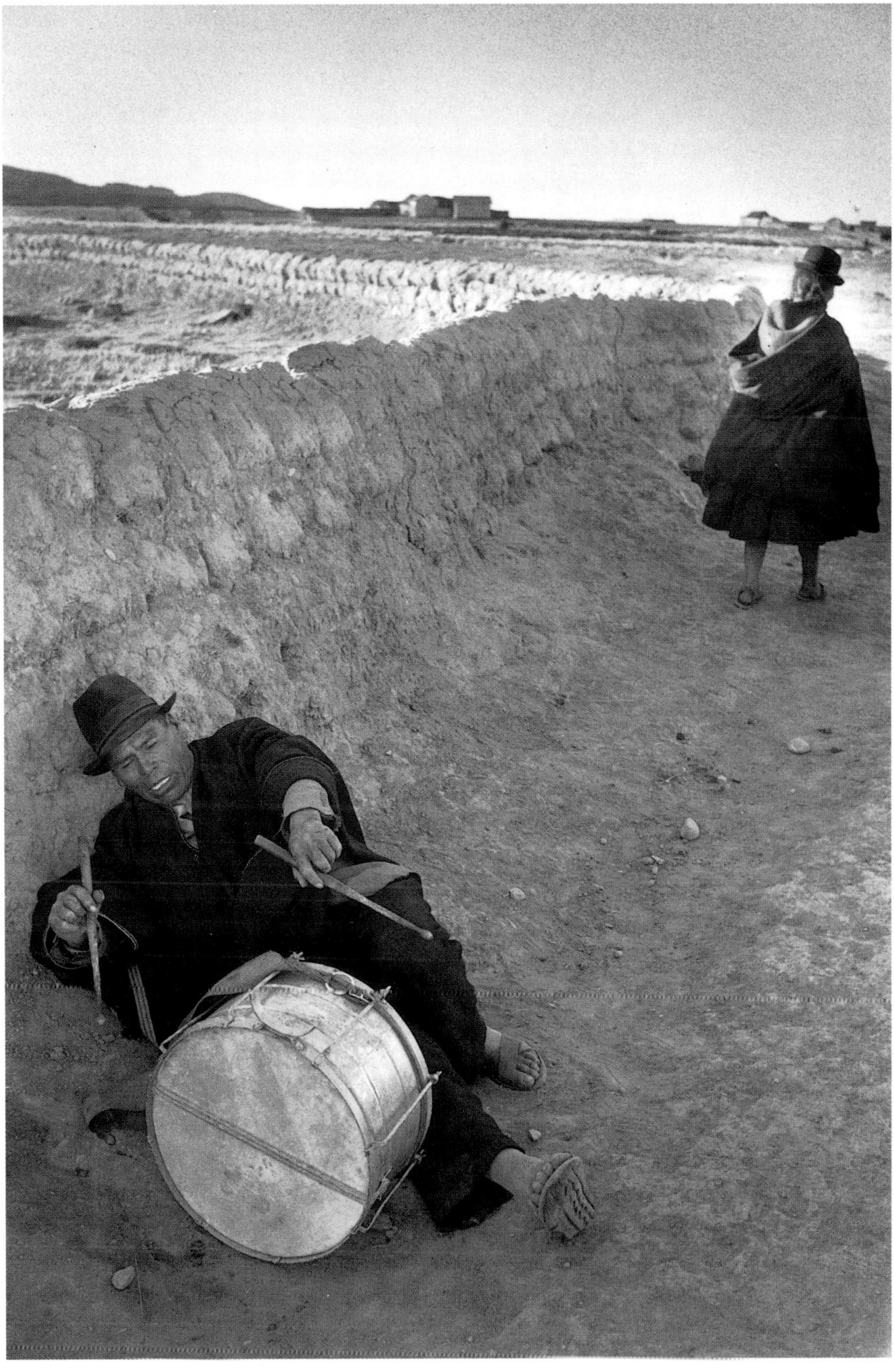

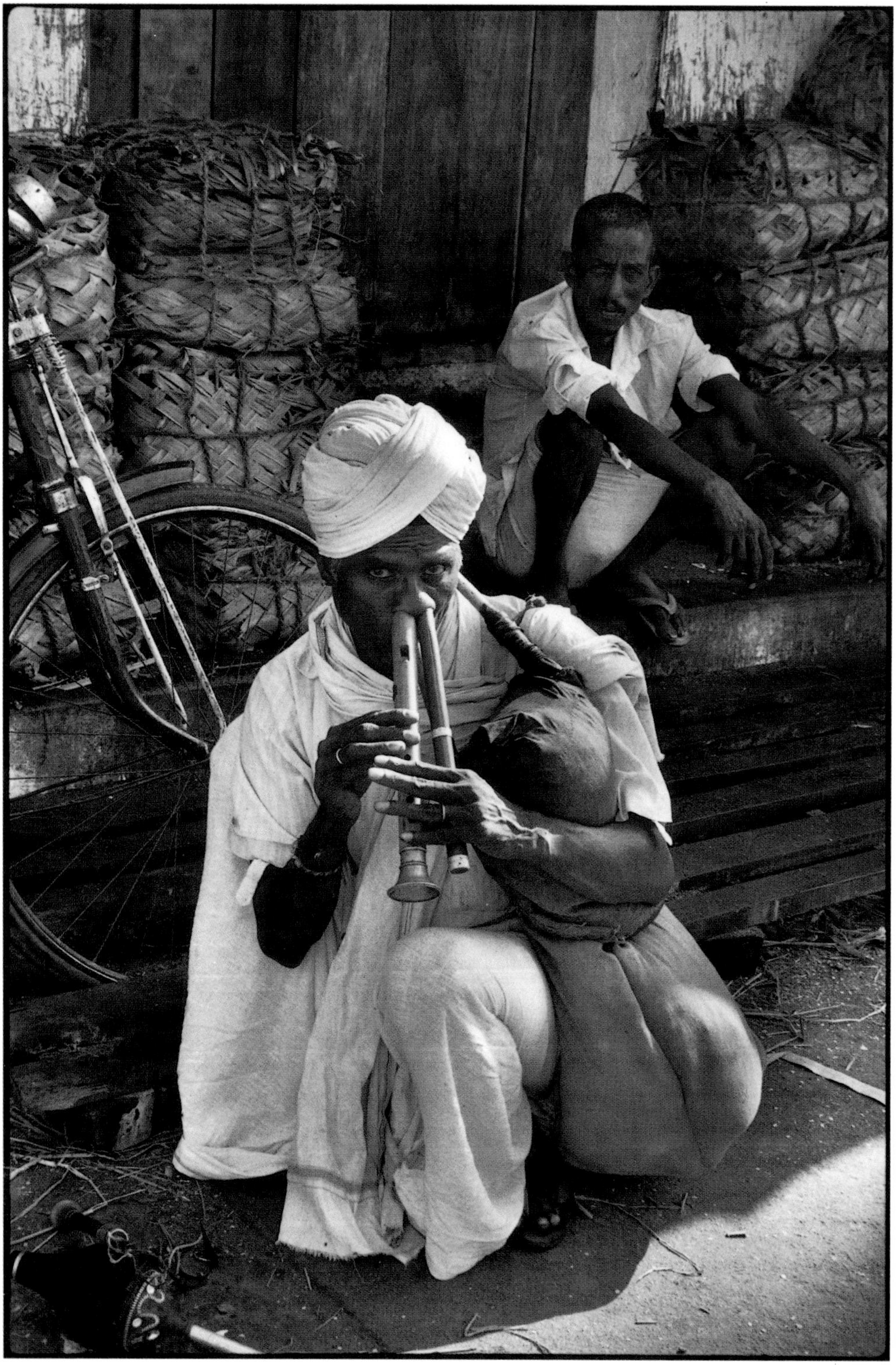

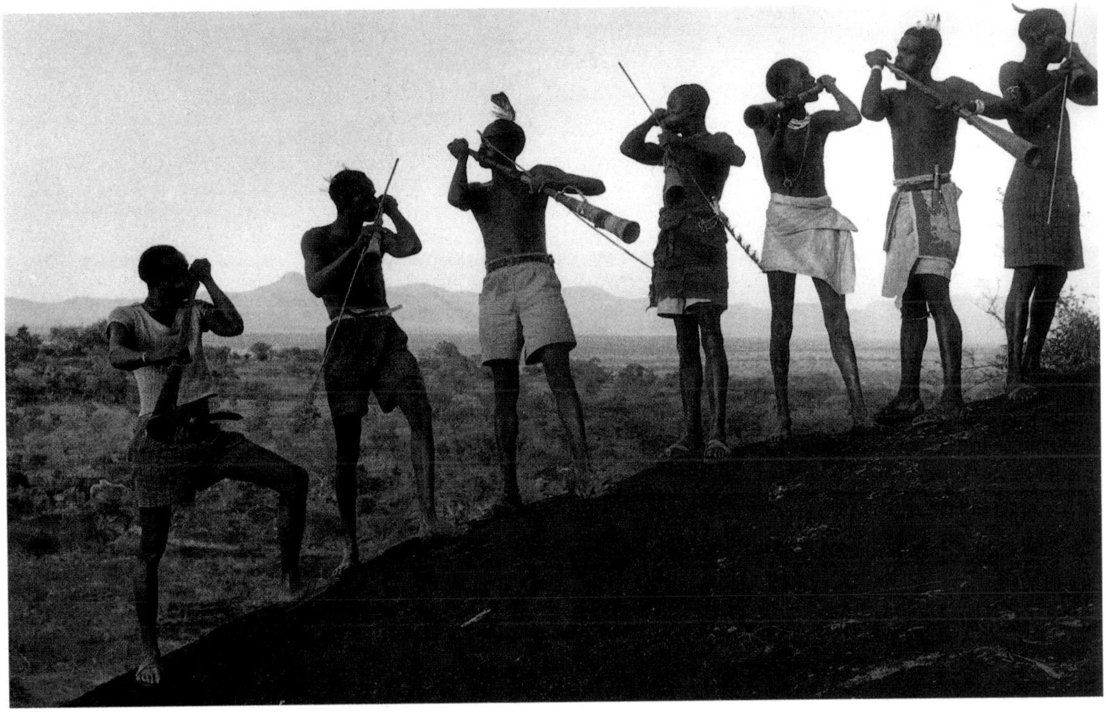

George Rodger
Kapore, Uganda, 1948.

Eve Arnold
Man playing nose flute, New Delhi, 1978.

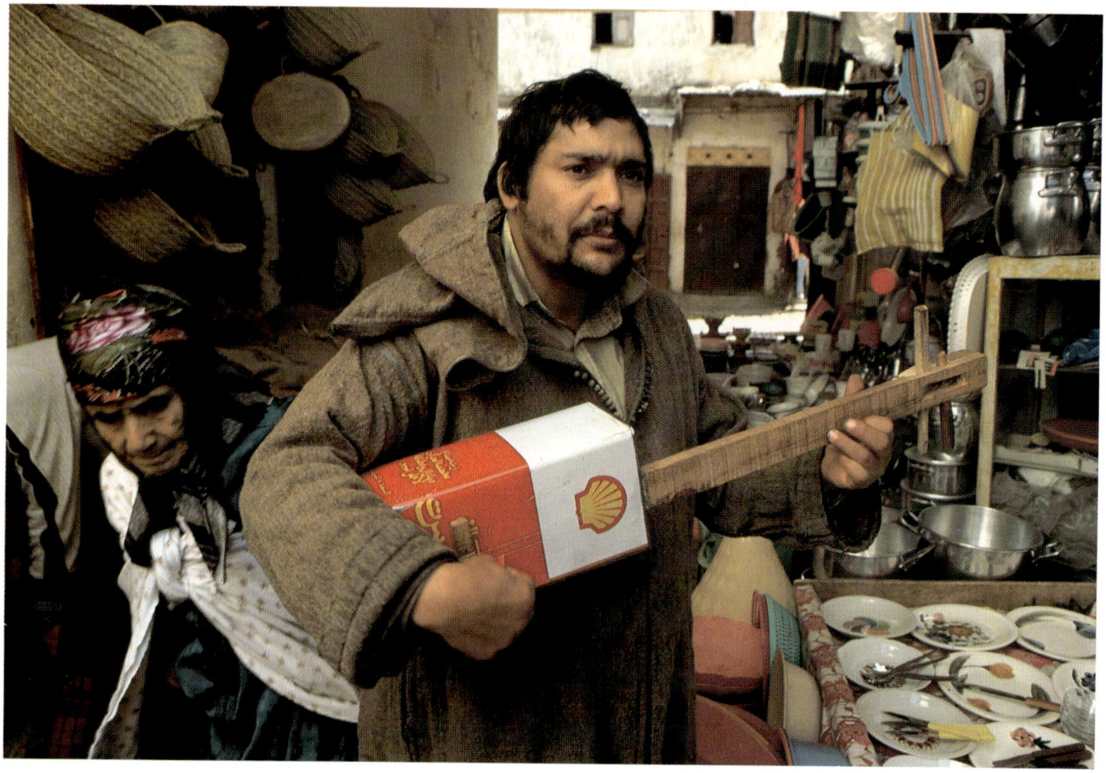

Bruno Barbey
Fez, Morocco, 1986.

René Burri
Japan, 1972.

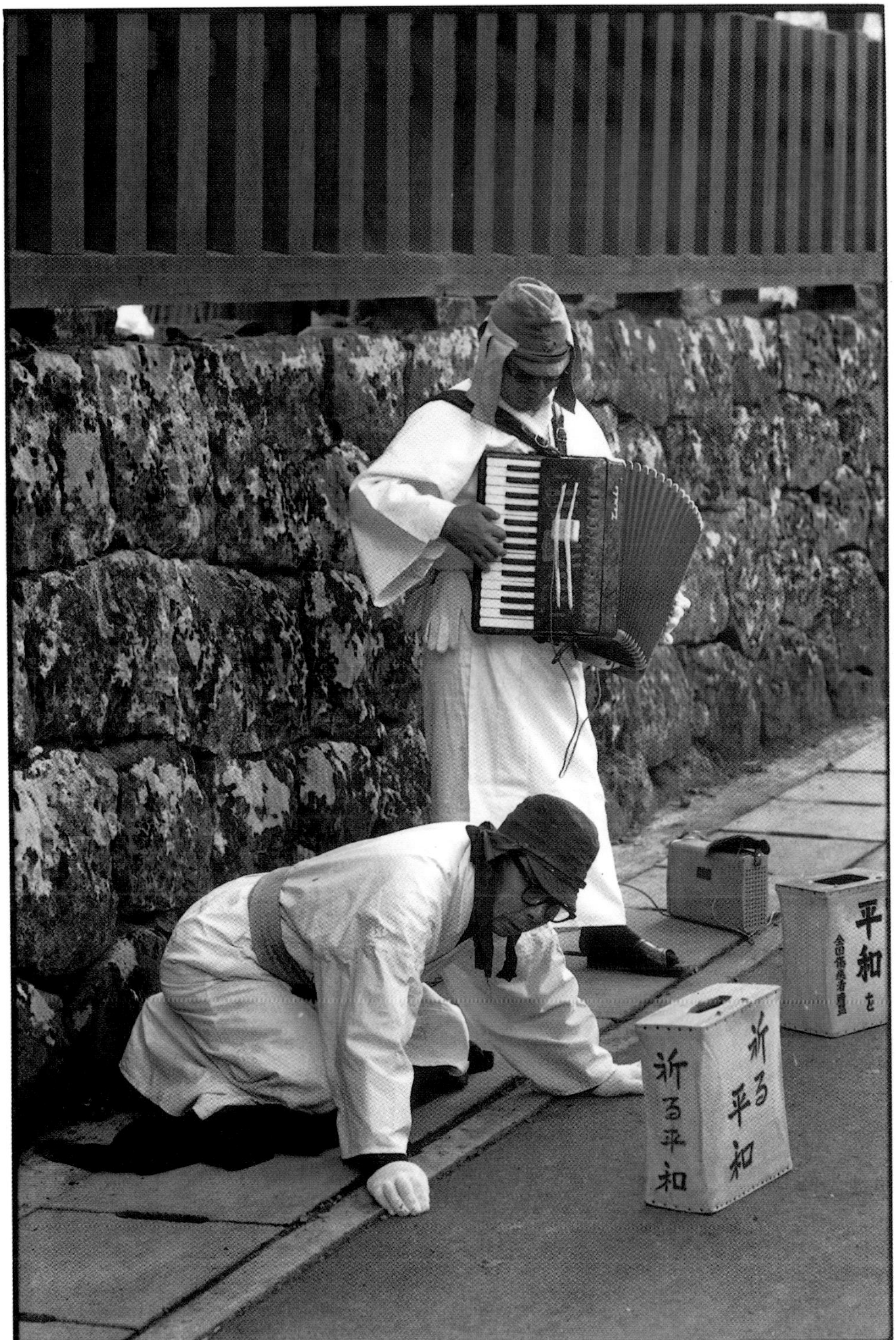

平和を
祈る平和
祈る平和

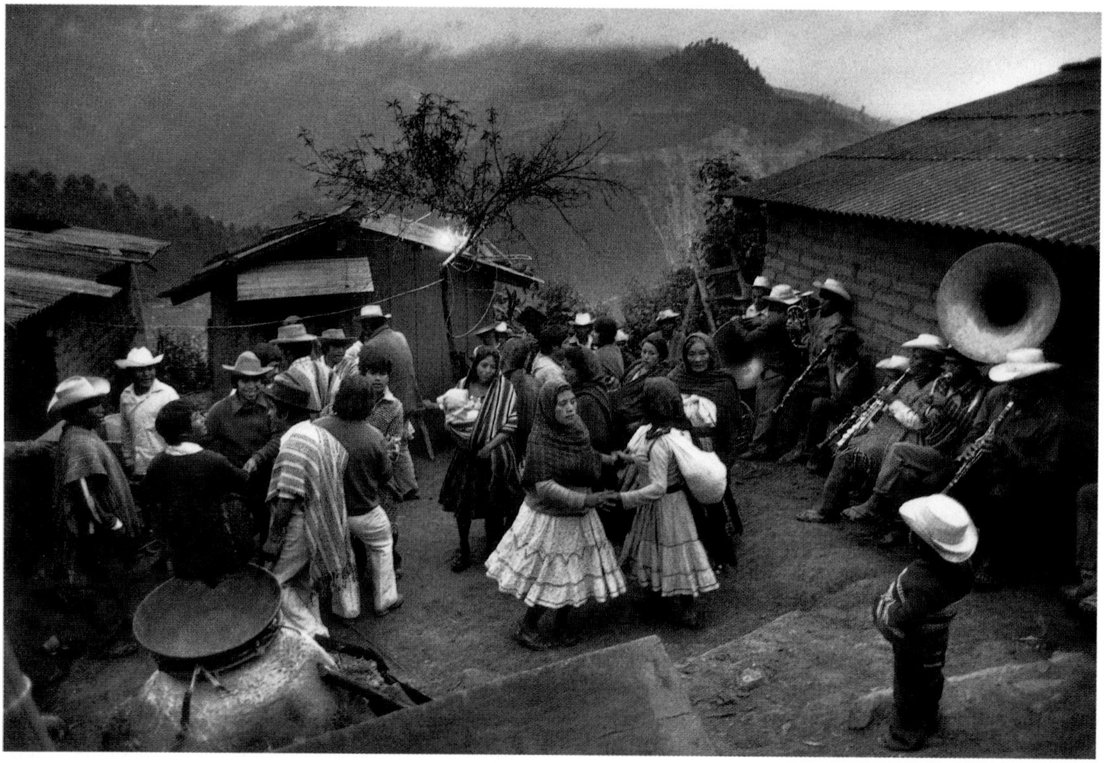

Sebastiao Salgado
Indian village,
Mexico, 1980.

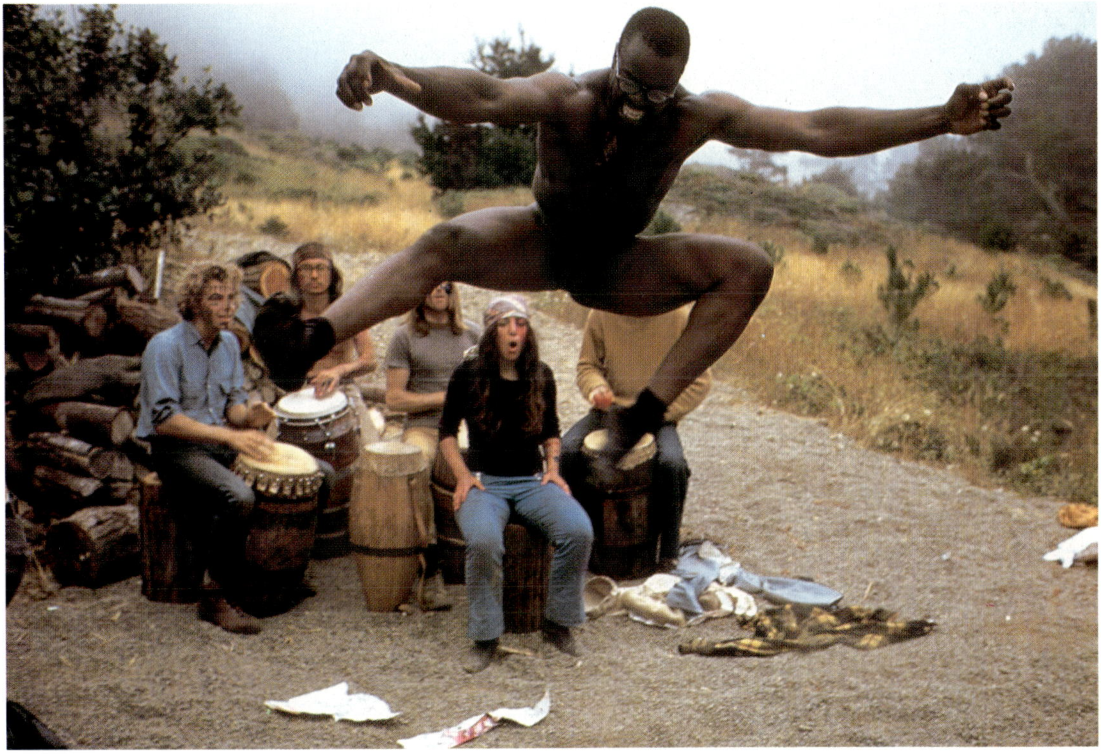

Paul Fusco
Hippy gathering, USA, 1969.

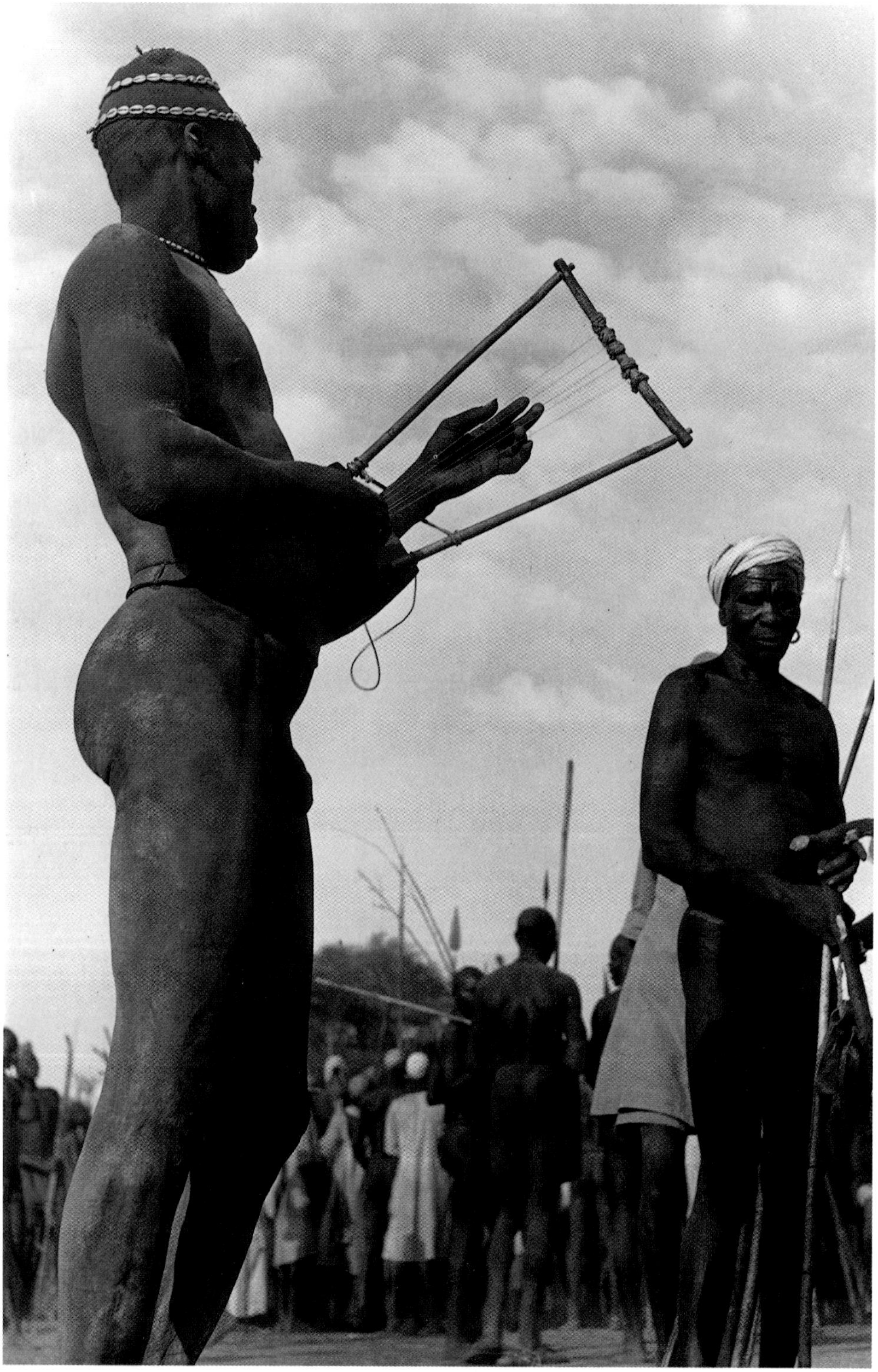

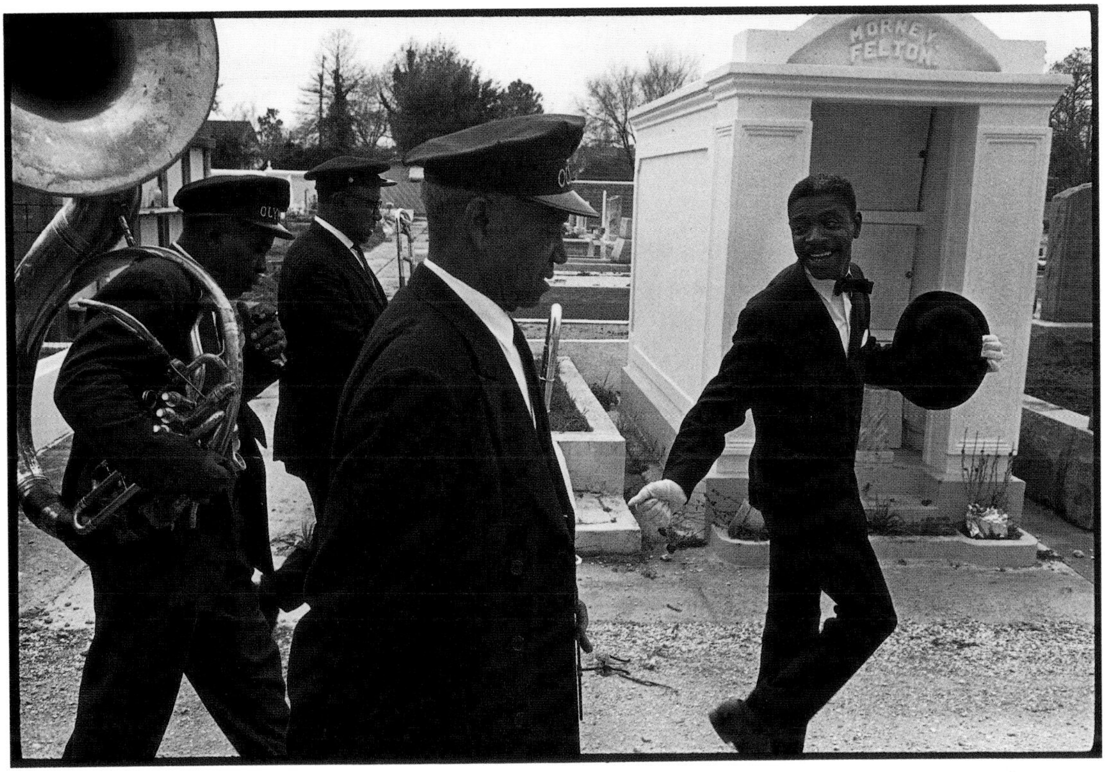

Leonard Freed
Jazz funeral,
New Orleans, 1952.

George Rodger
Nuba musicians,
Sudan, 1949.

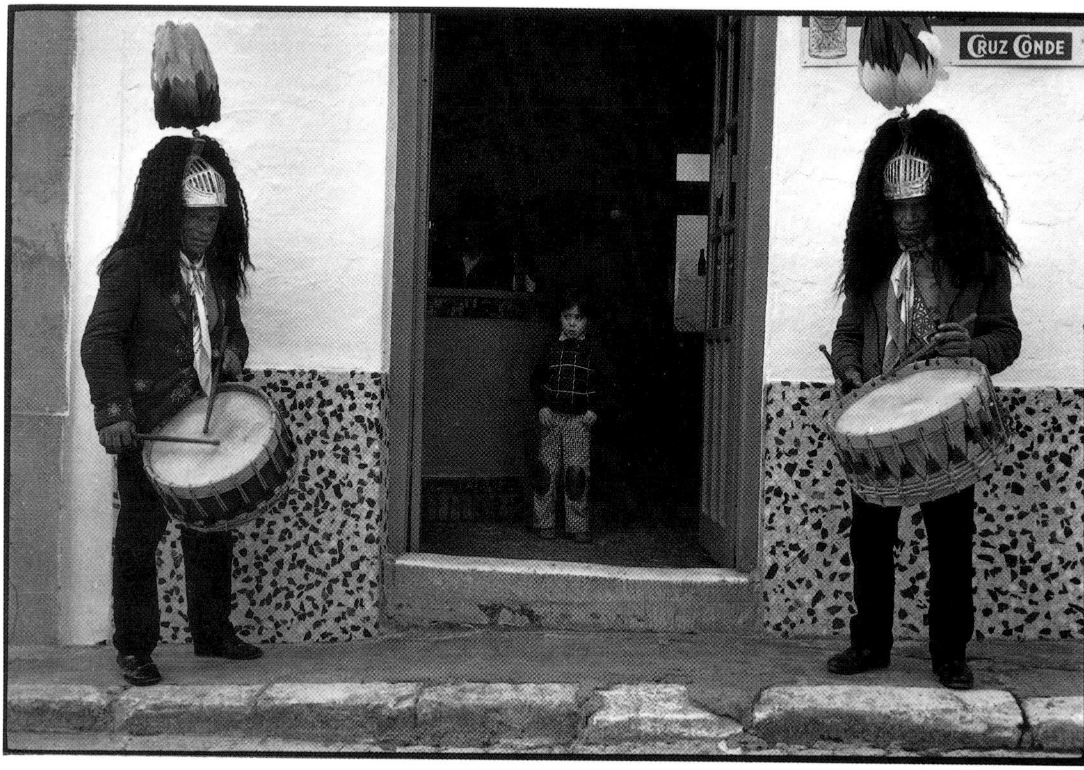

Josef Koudelka
Baena, Andalusia, Spain.

Bruno Barbey
Bastille Day, in Papeete, Tahiti, 1977.

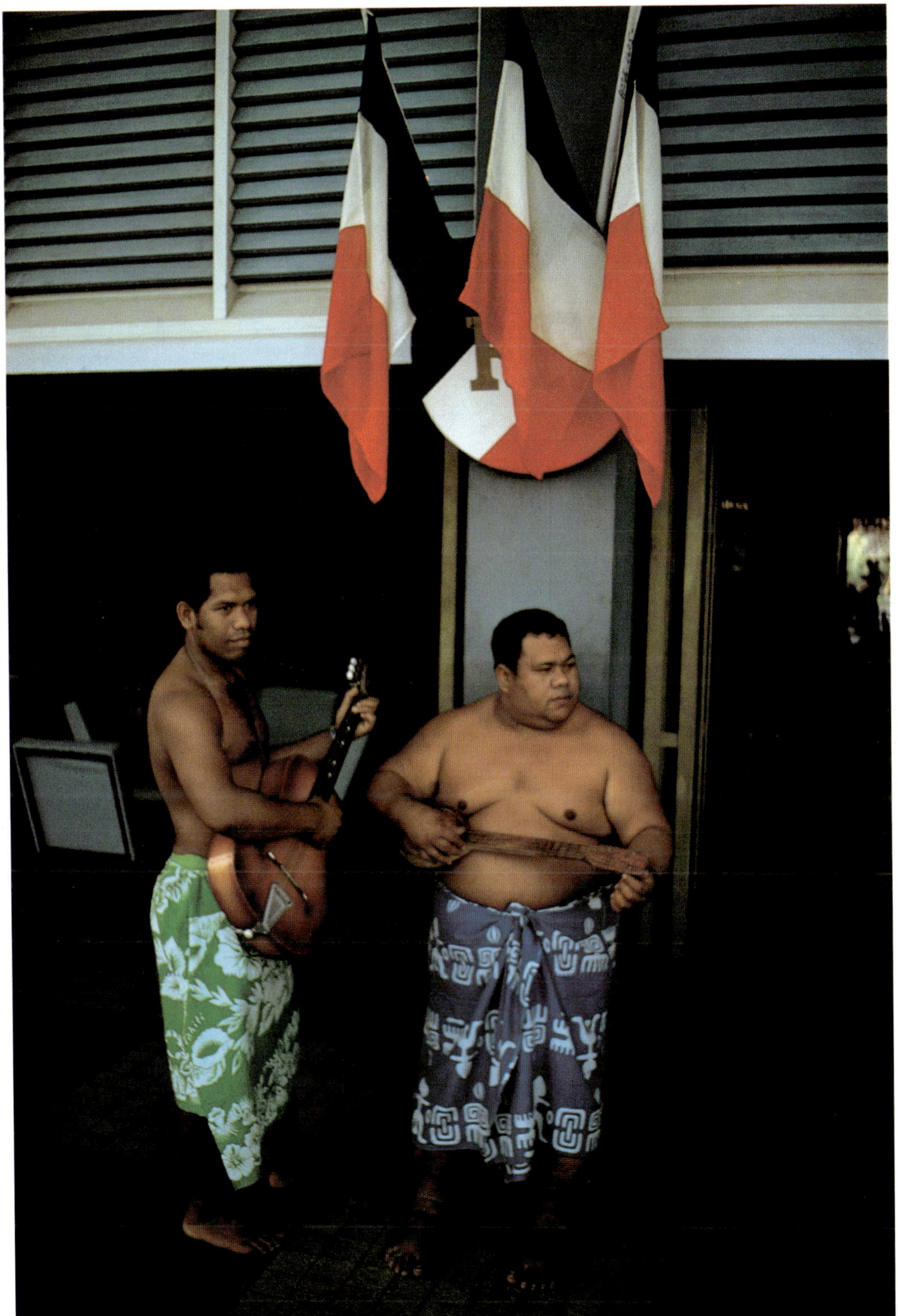

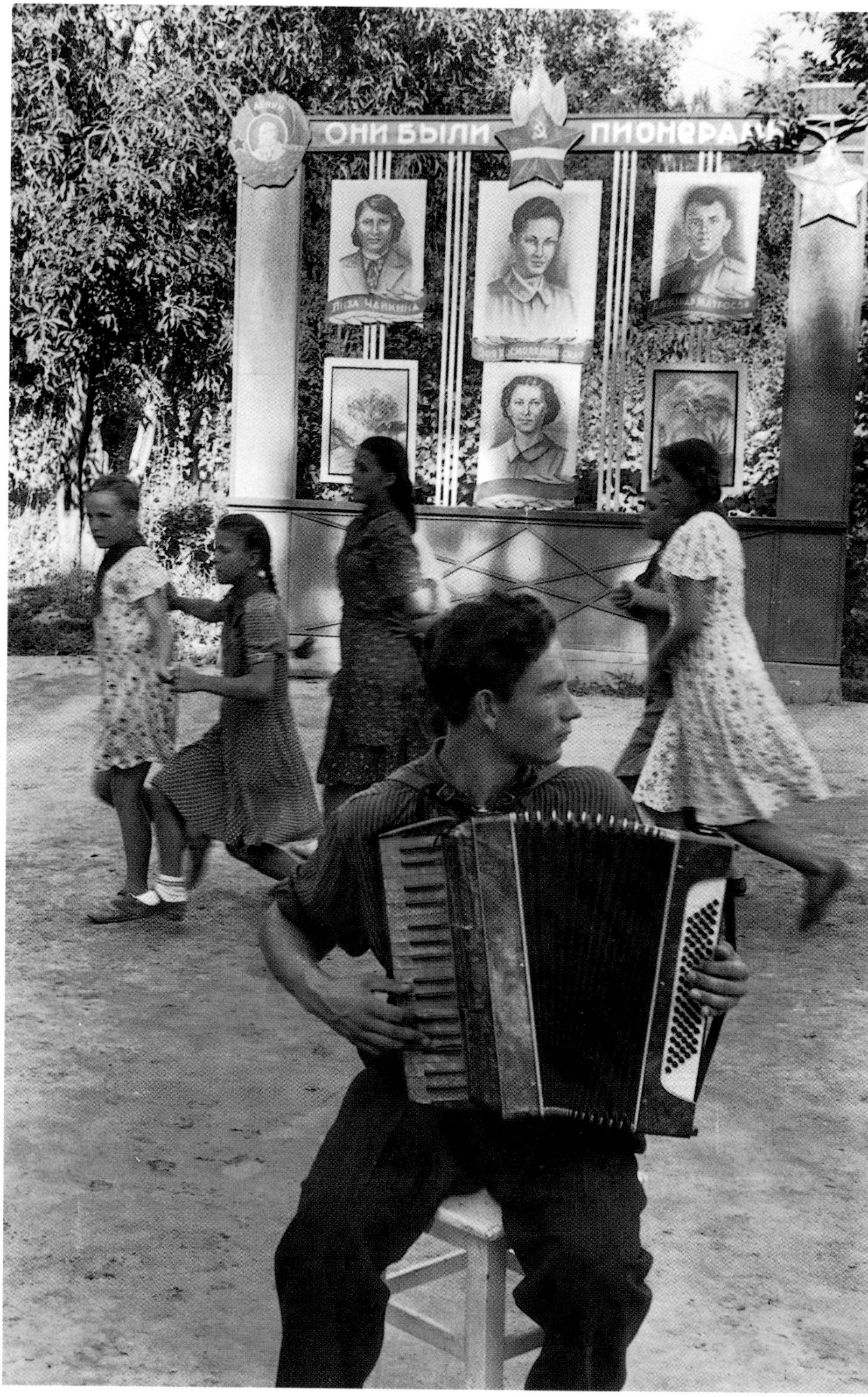
ОНИ БЫЛИ
ЛИЗА ЧАЙКИНА

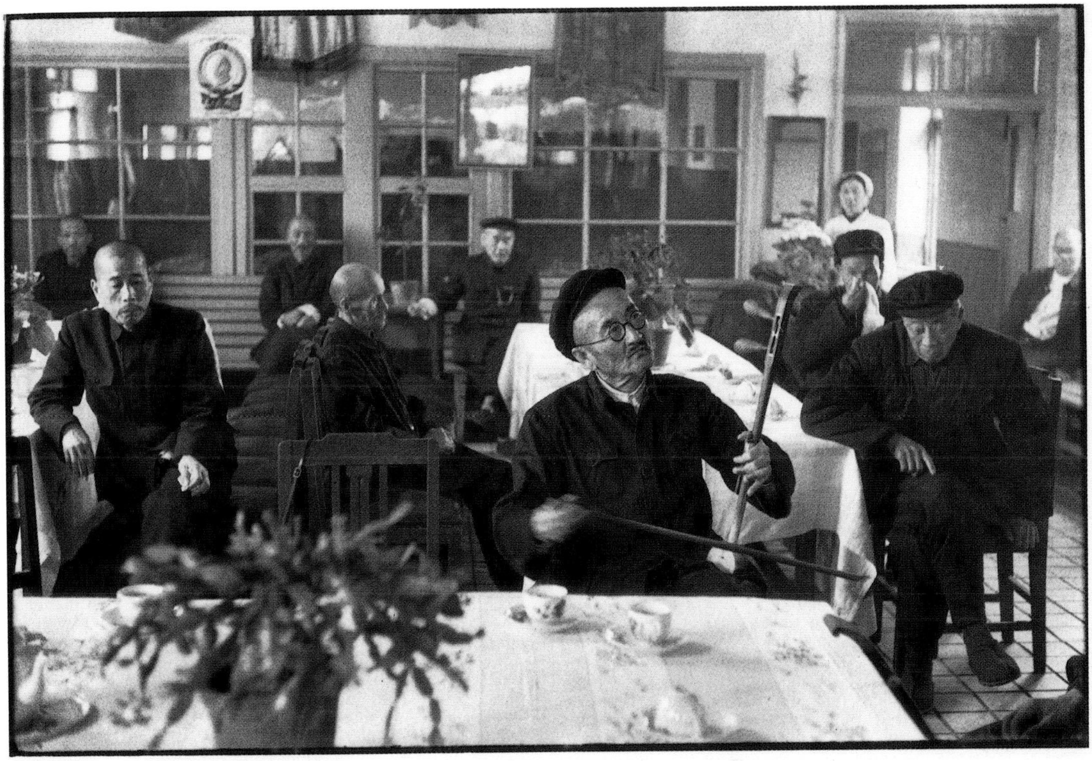

Marc Riboud
Home for the elderly,
China, 1957.

Henri Cartier-Bresson
Pioneers' Festival,
Moscow Culture Park, 1954.

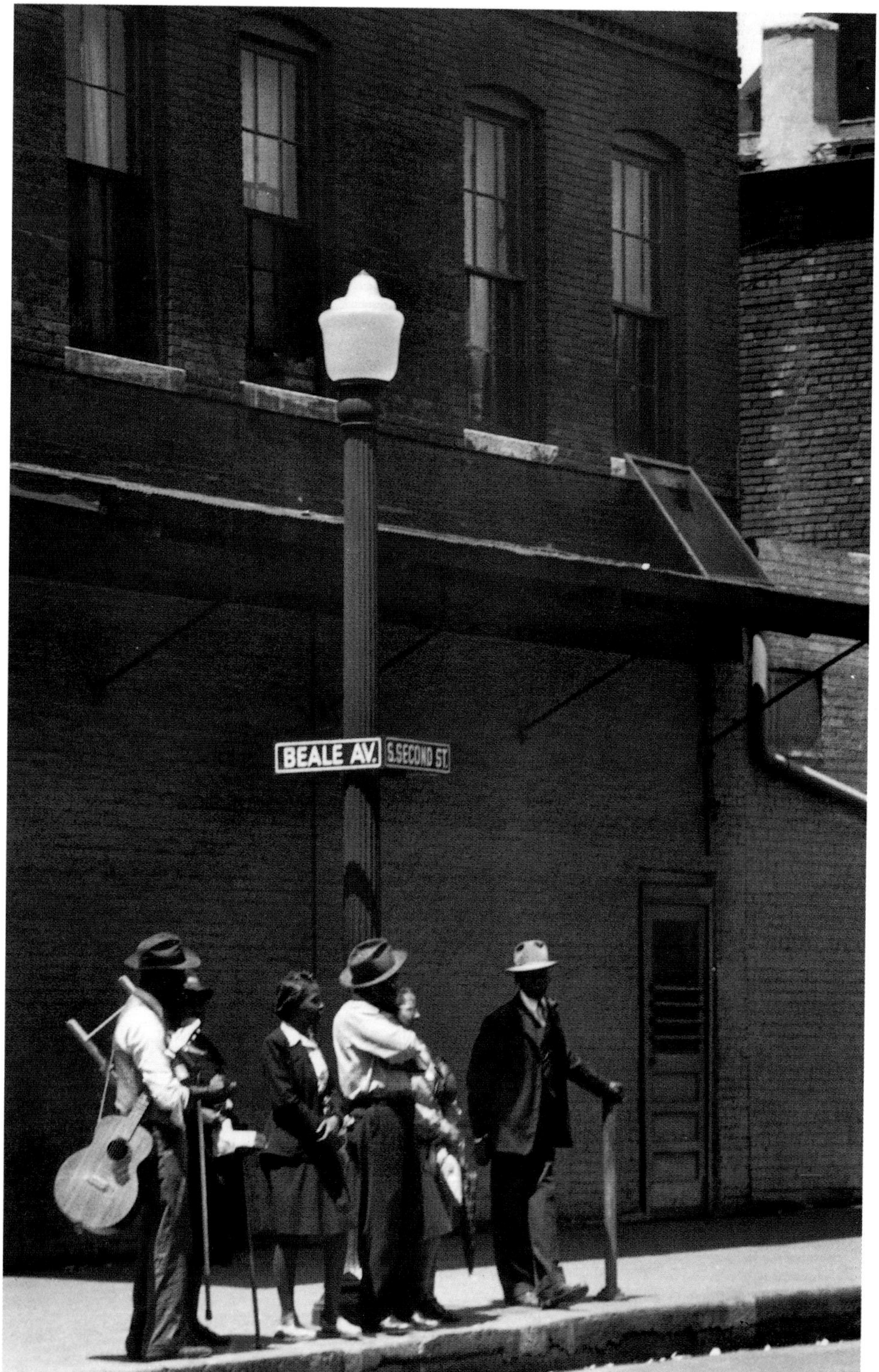
BEALE AV.
S.SECOND ST.

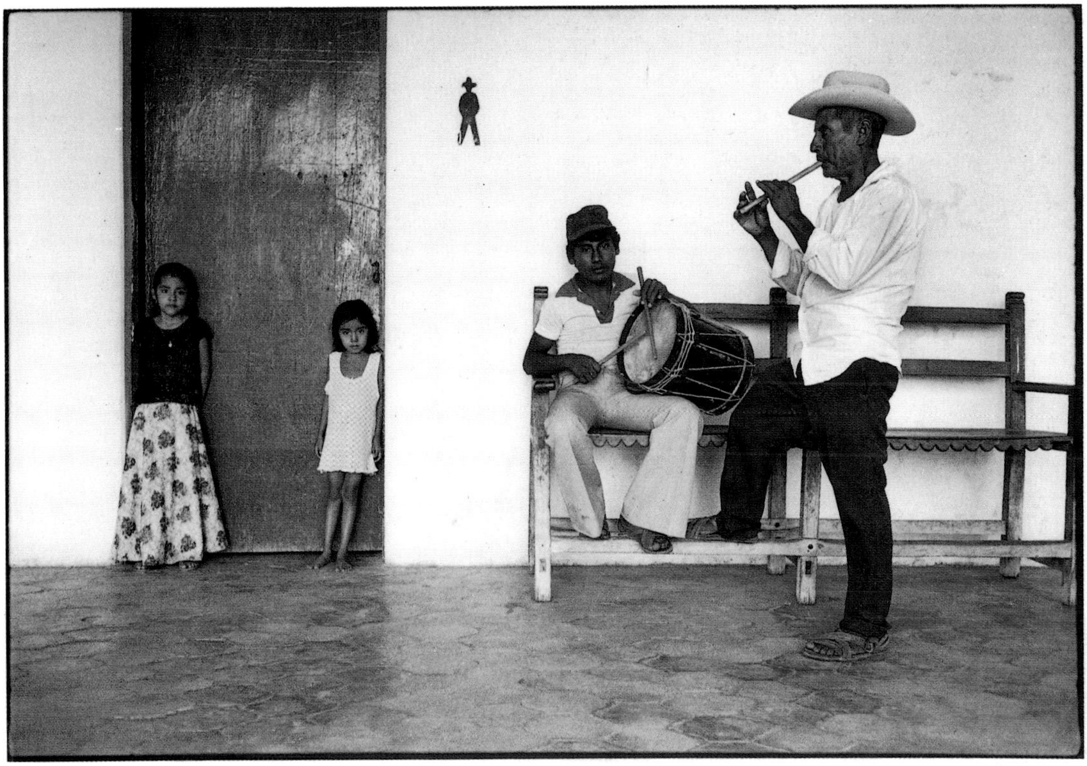

Sebastiao Salgado
Istmo de Teuantepec, Mexico, 1981.

Henri Cartier-Bresson
New Orleans, USA.

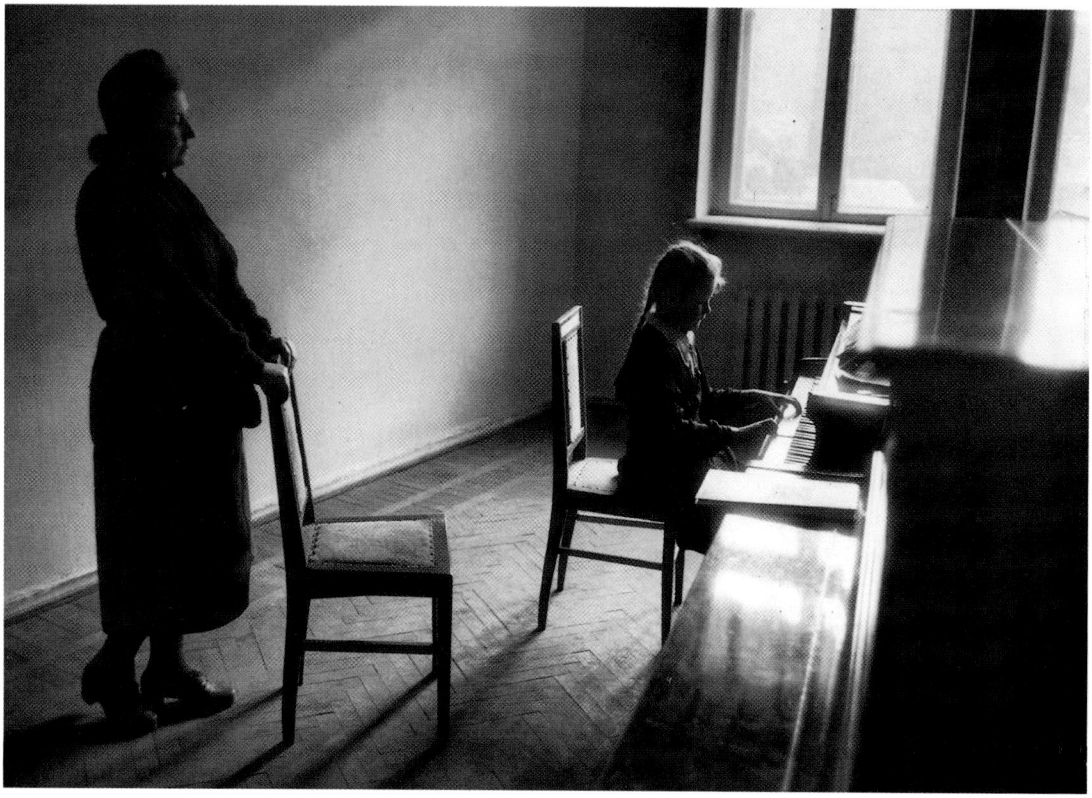

Elliott Erwitt
Conservatory School,
Odessa, USSR, 1957.

Bruce Davidson
Leonard Bernstein,
1958.

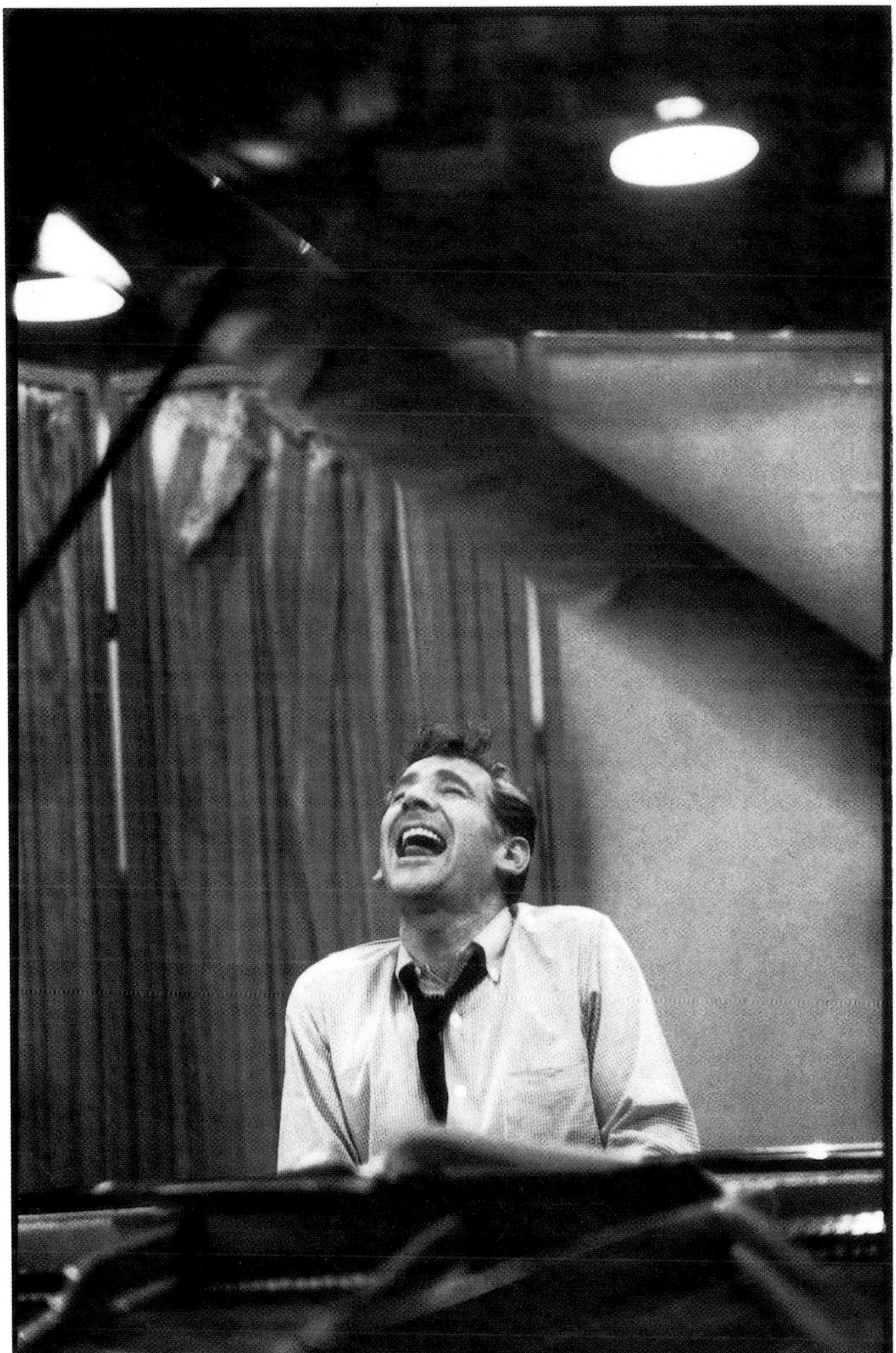

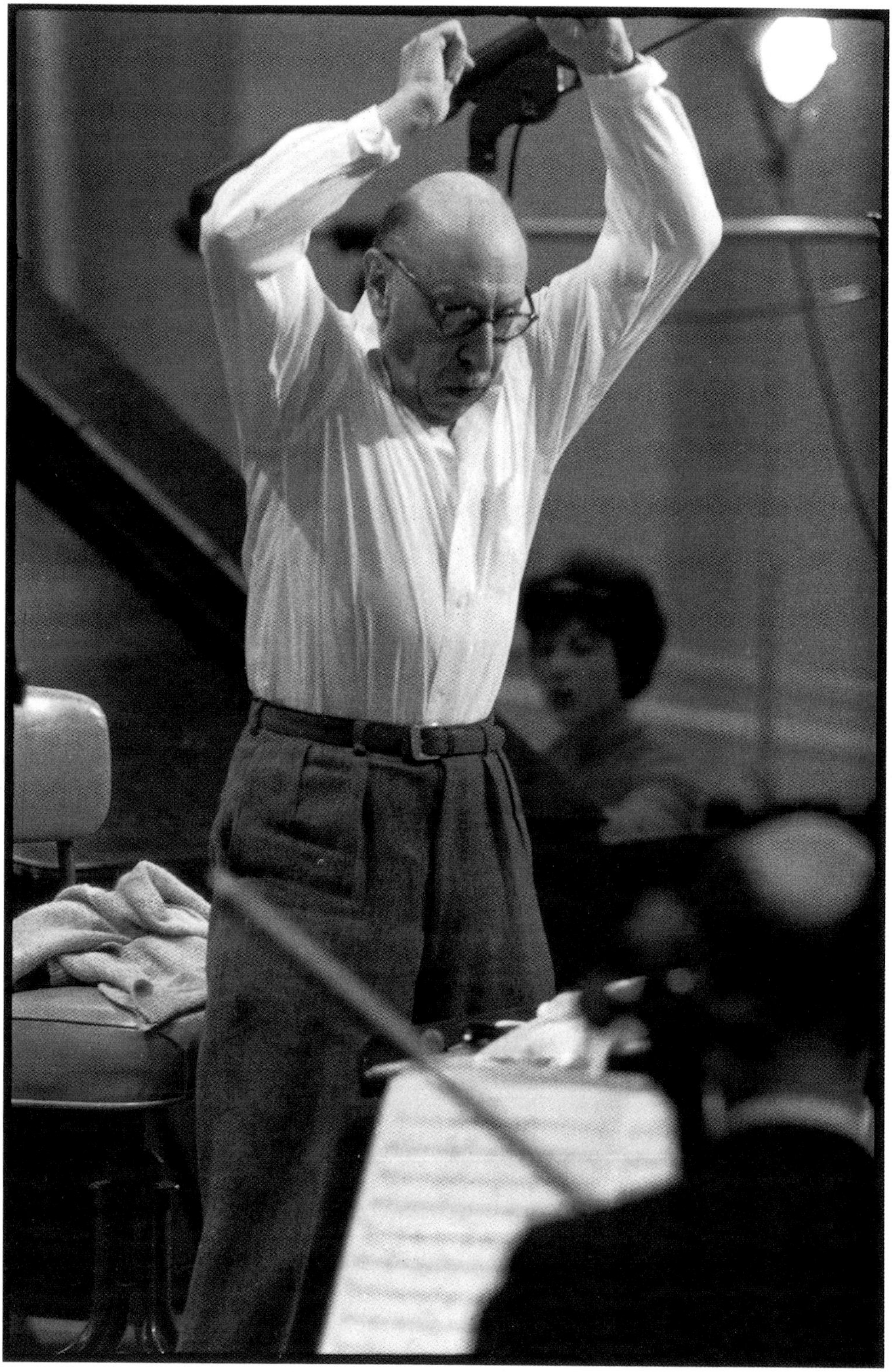

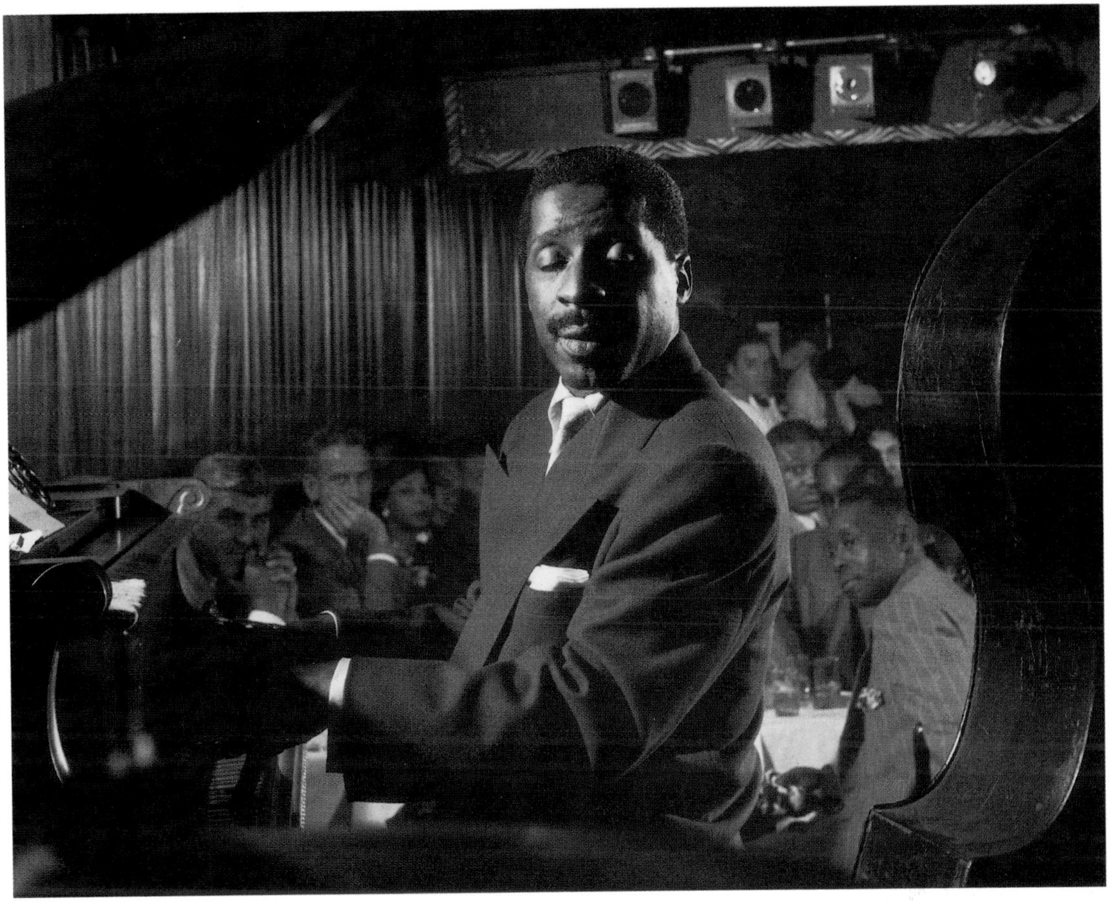

Dennis Stock
Errol Garner at the Three Deuces, New York.

Ernst Haas
Igor Stravinsky, 1962.

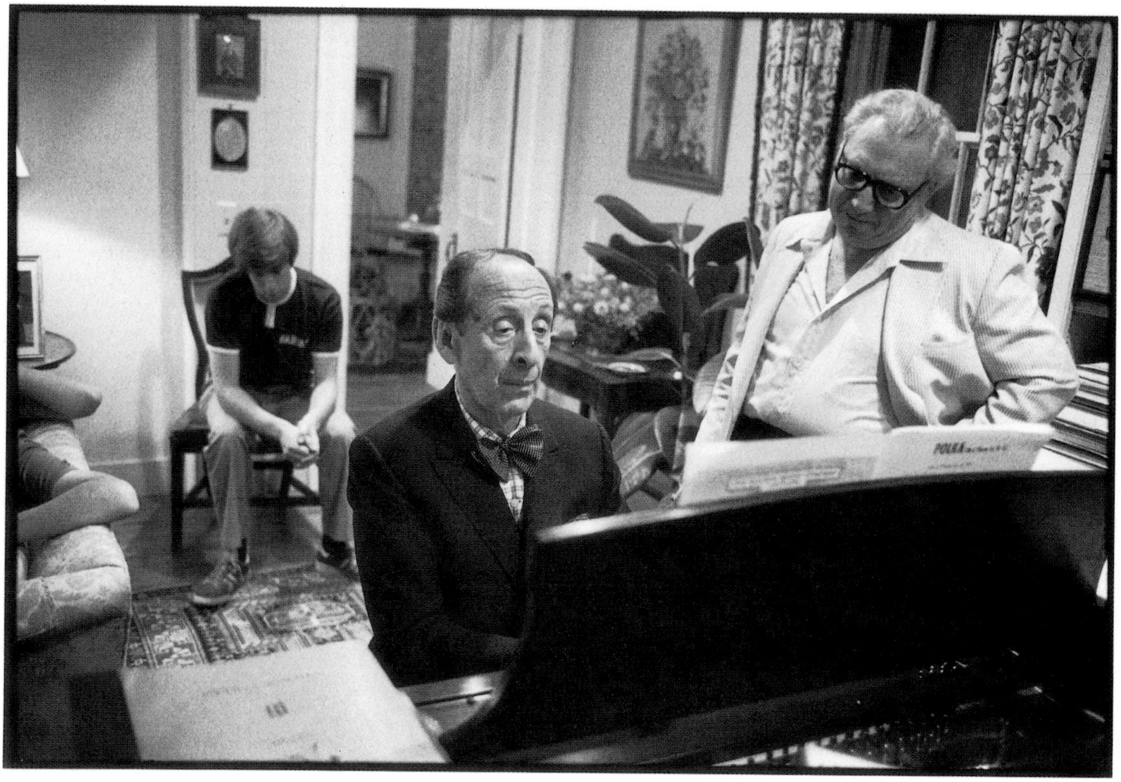

Inge Morath
Isaac Stern & Vladimir Horowitz, 1977.

Elliott Erwitt
Sarah Caldwell, 1975.

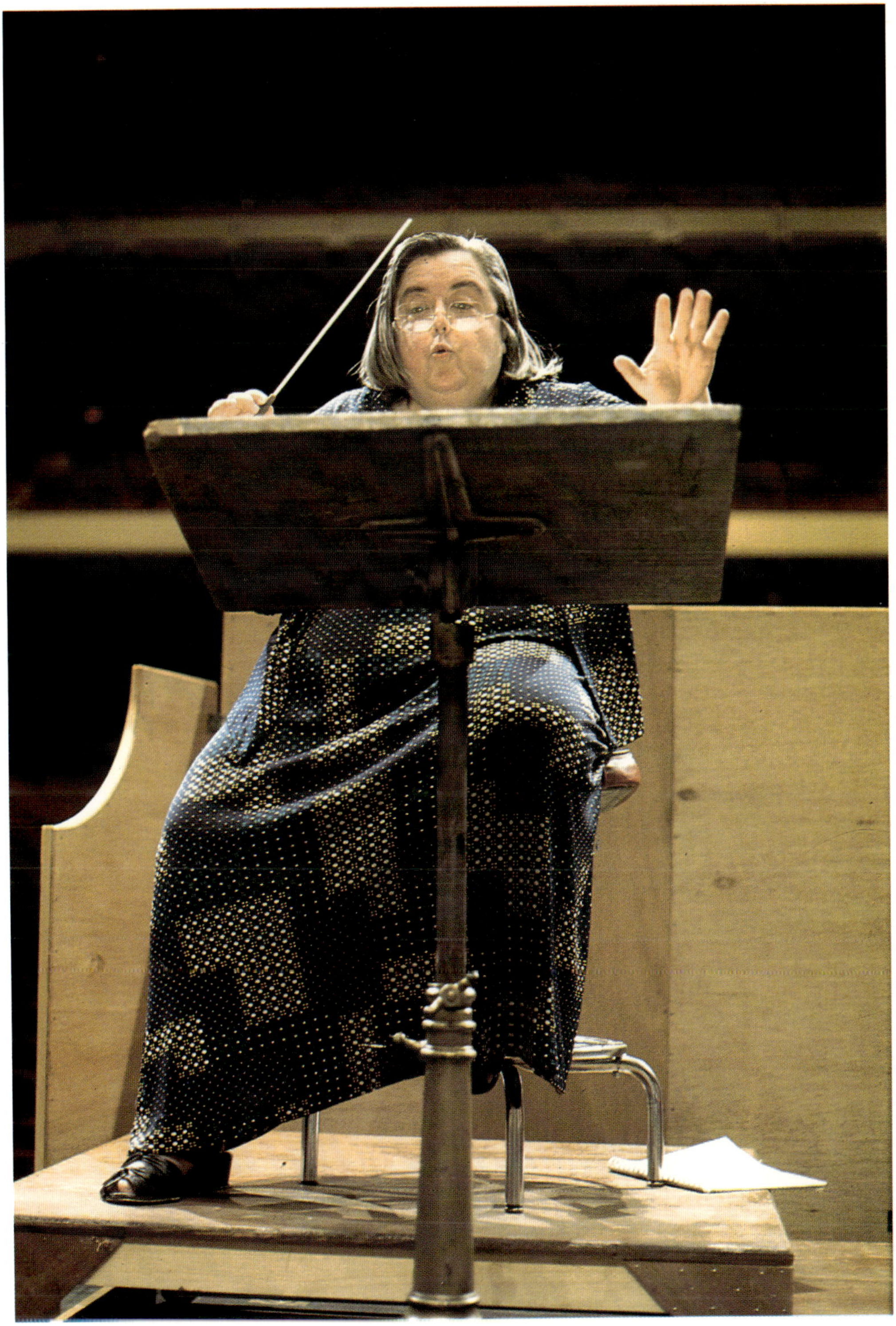

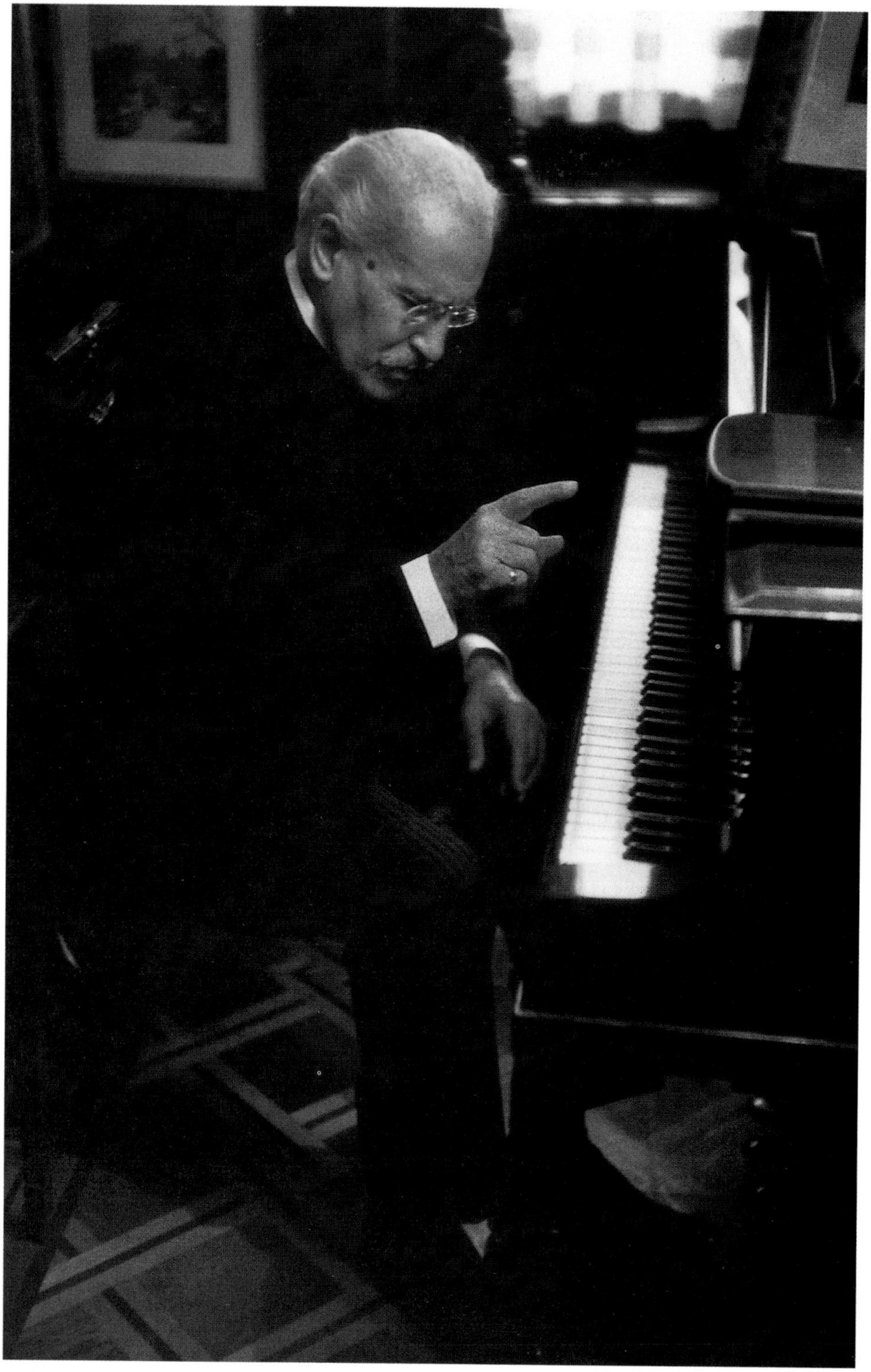

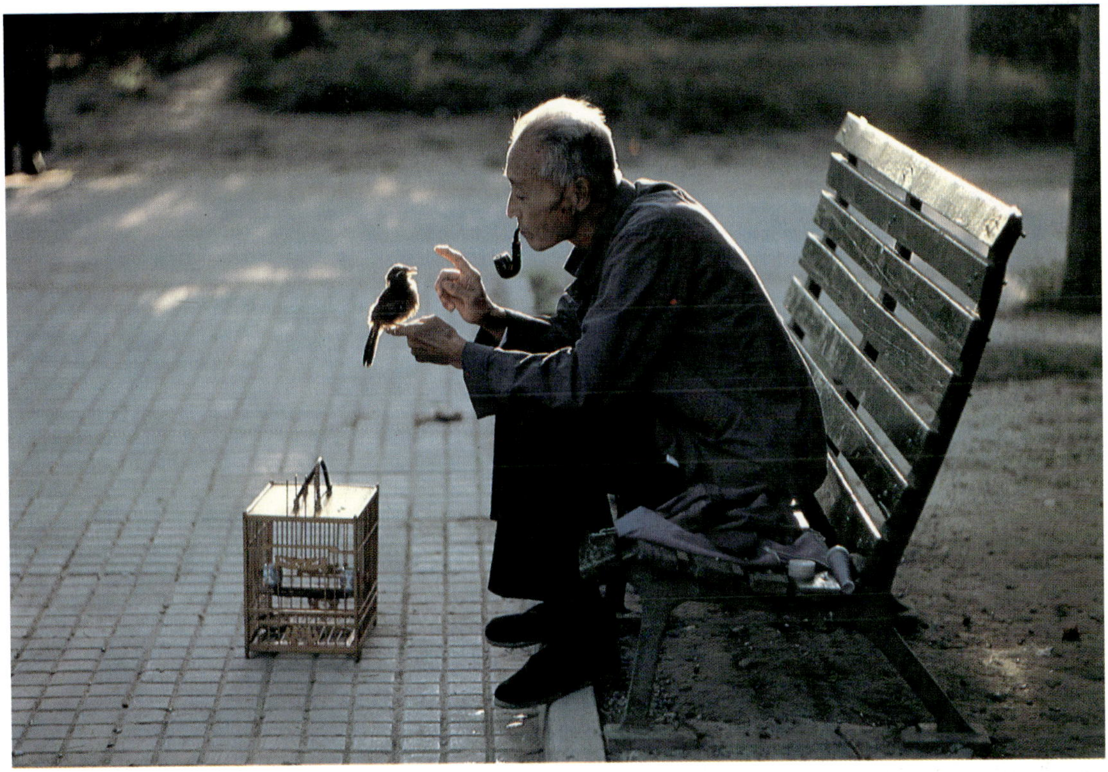

Thomas Hoepker
Ritan Park, Peking,
1985.

David Seymour
Arturo Toscanini,
1954.

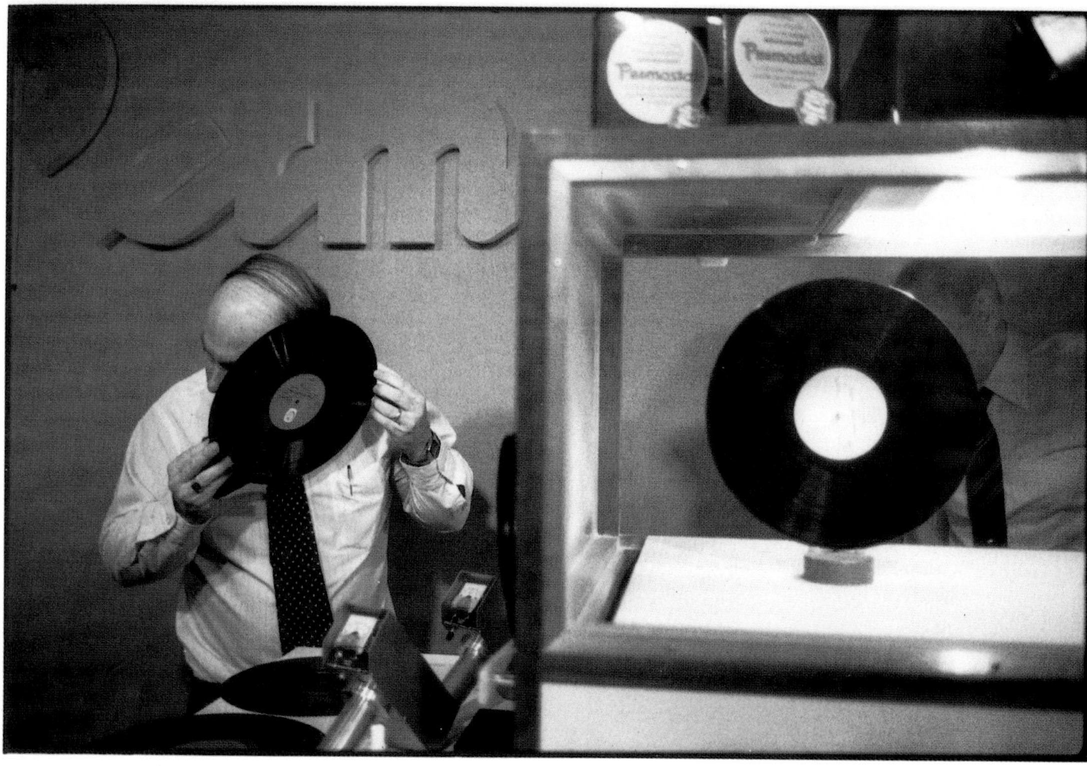

Guy Le Querrec
'Festival of Sound',
Paris, 1980.

René Burri
Robot playing the organ,
Tsukuba International Exhibition,
Japan, 1985.

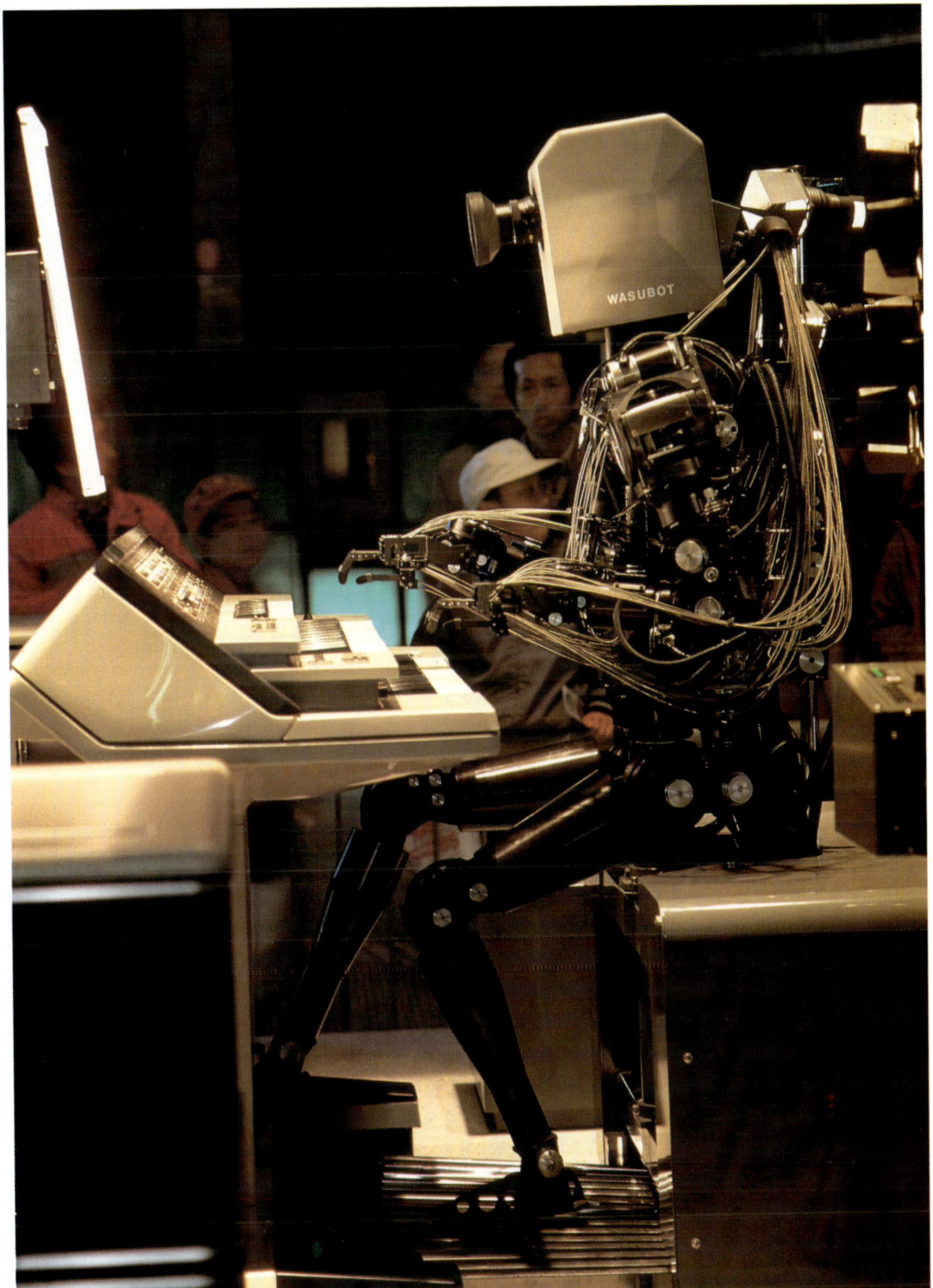
WASUBOT

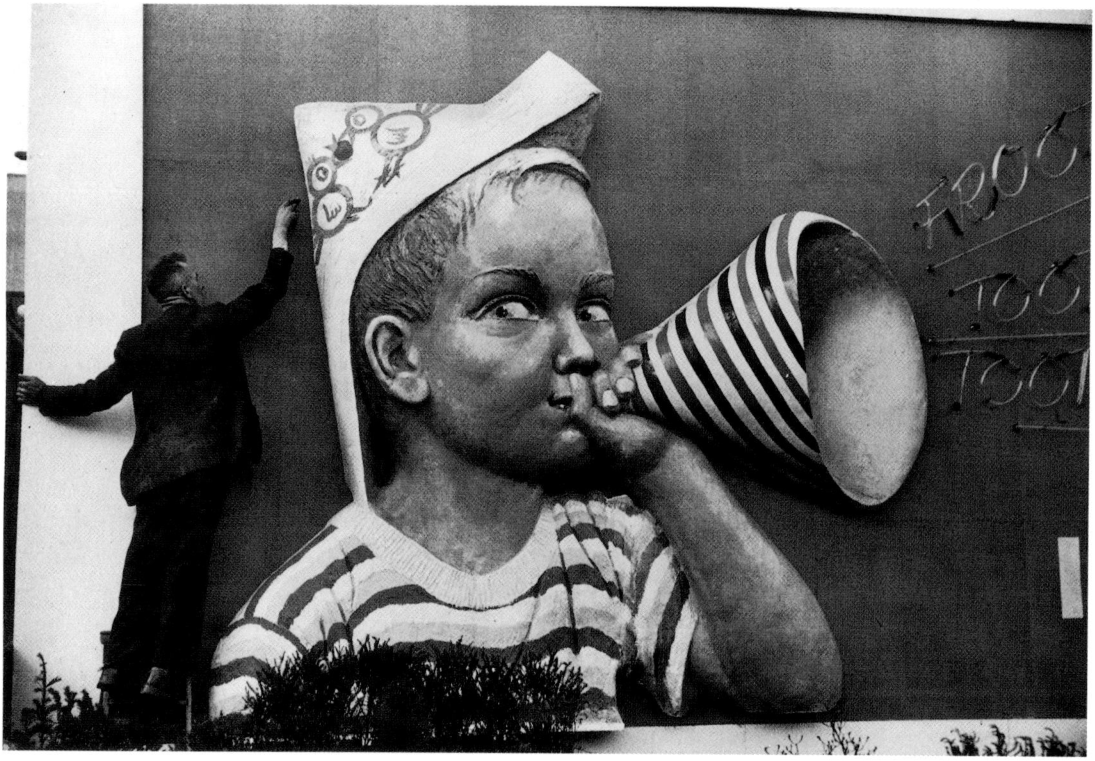

Marc Riboud
Untitled.

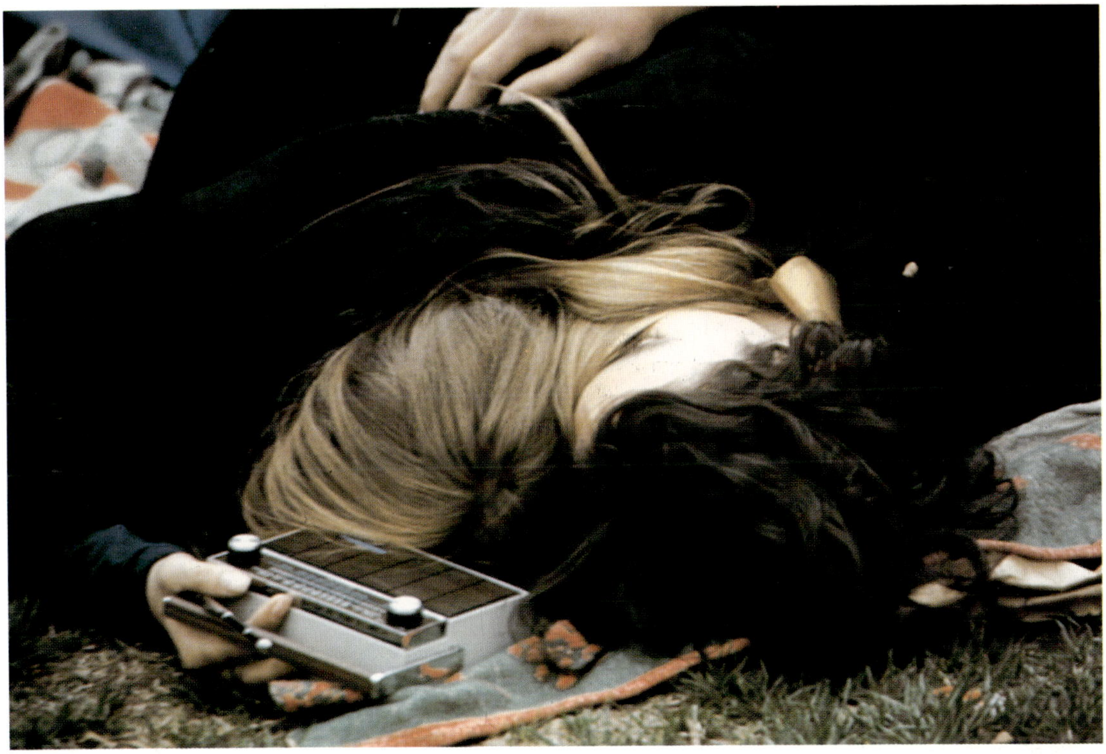

Cornell Capa
Central Park,
New York, 1976.

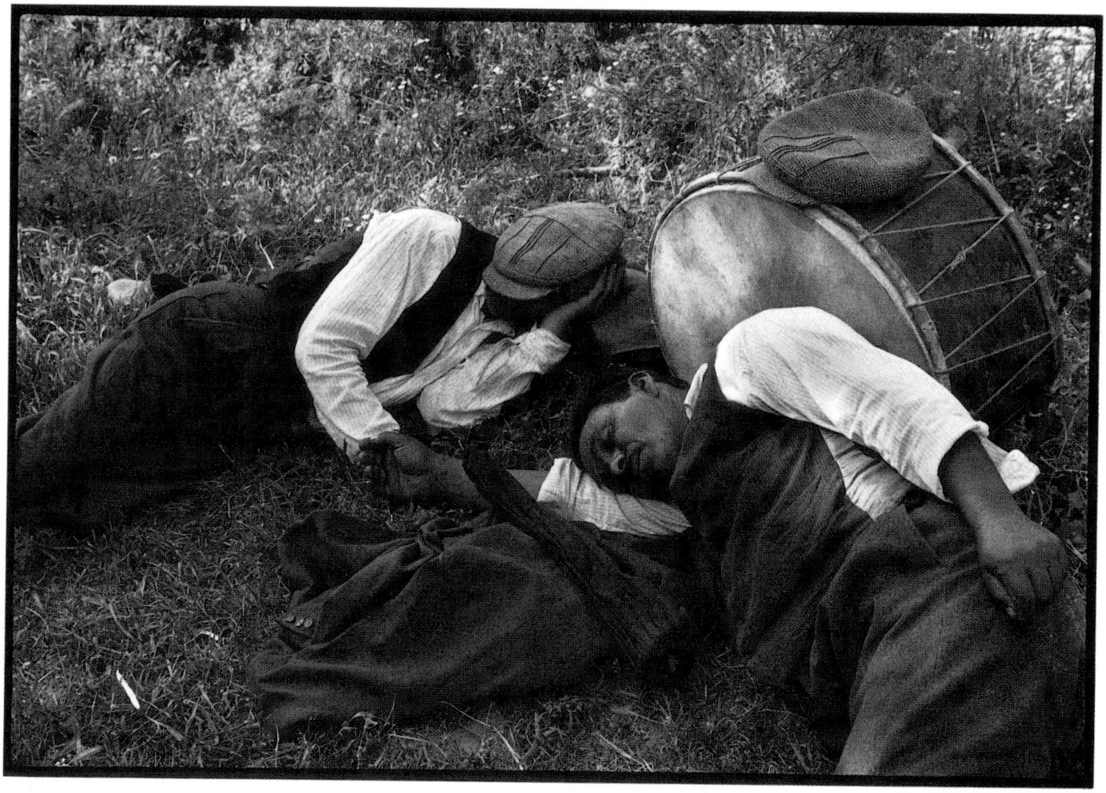

Costa Manos
Sleeping musicians,
Makedhonia, Greece, 1964.

Josef Koudelka
Local fair,
Czechoslovakia.

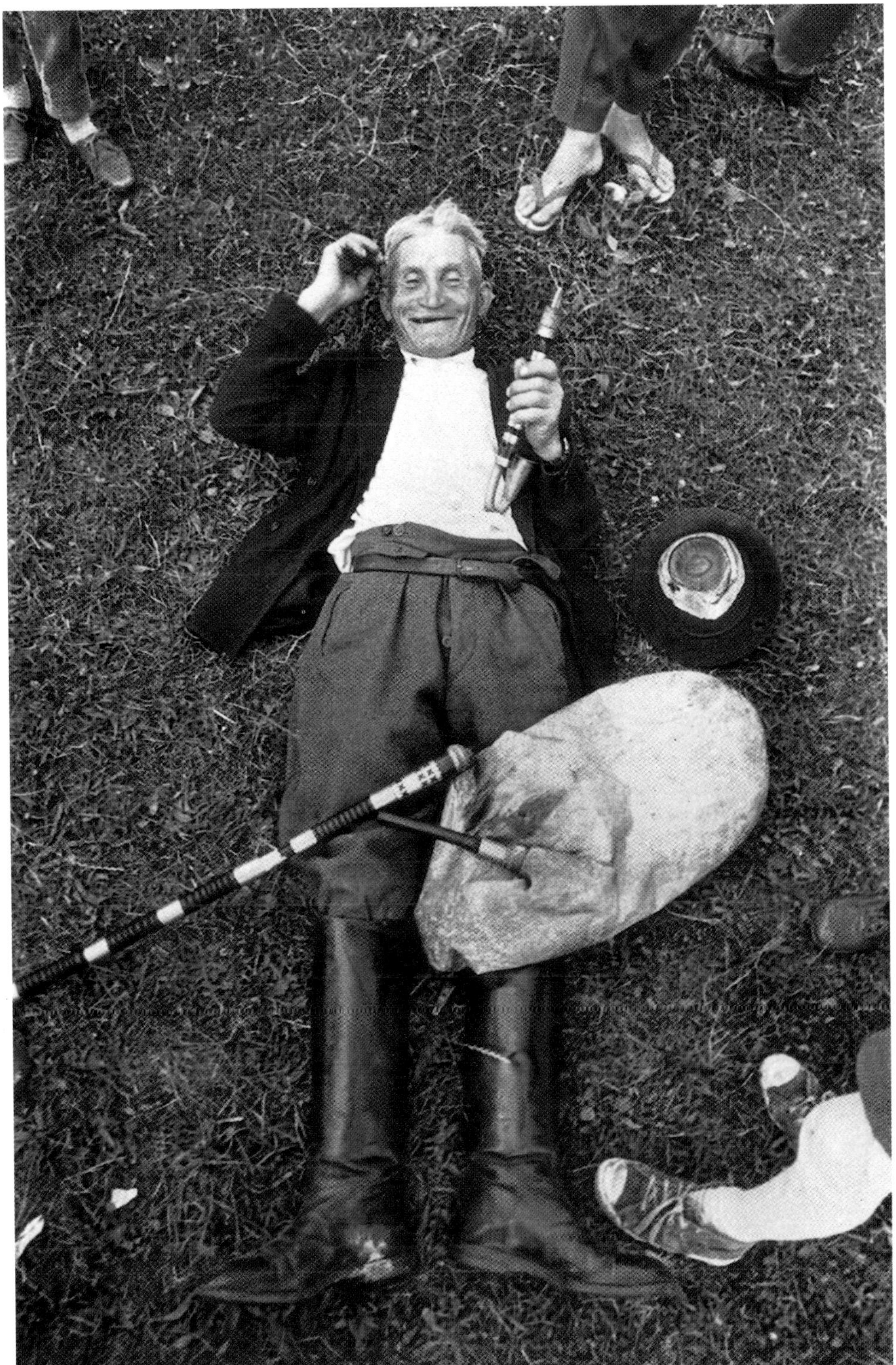

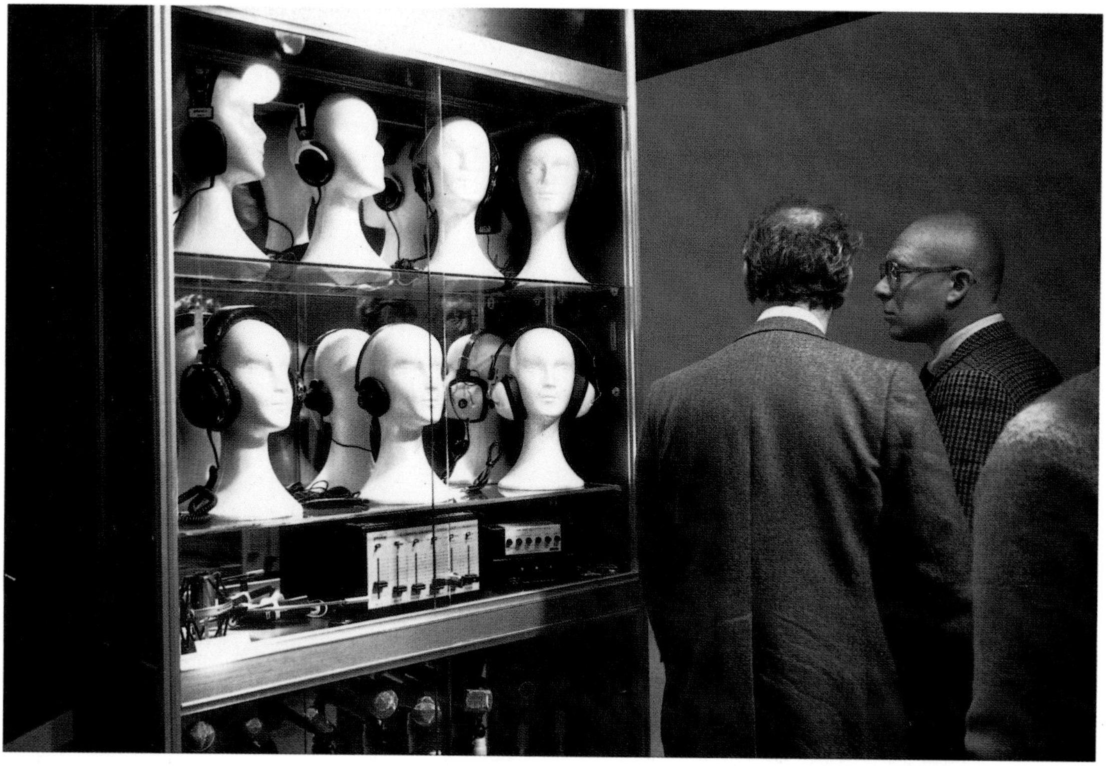

Guy Le Querrec
'Festival of Sound',
Paris, 1980.

René Burri
Oman, 1975.

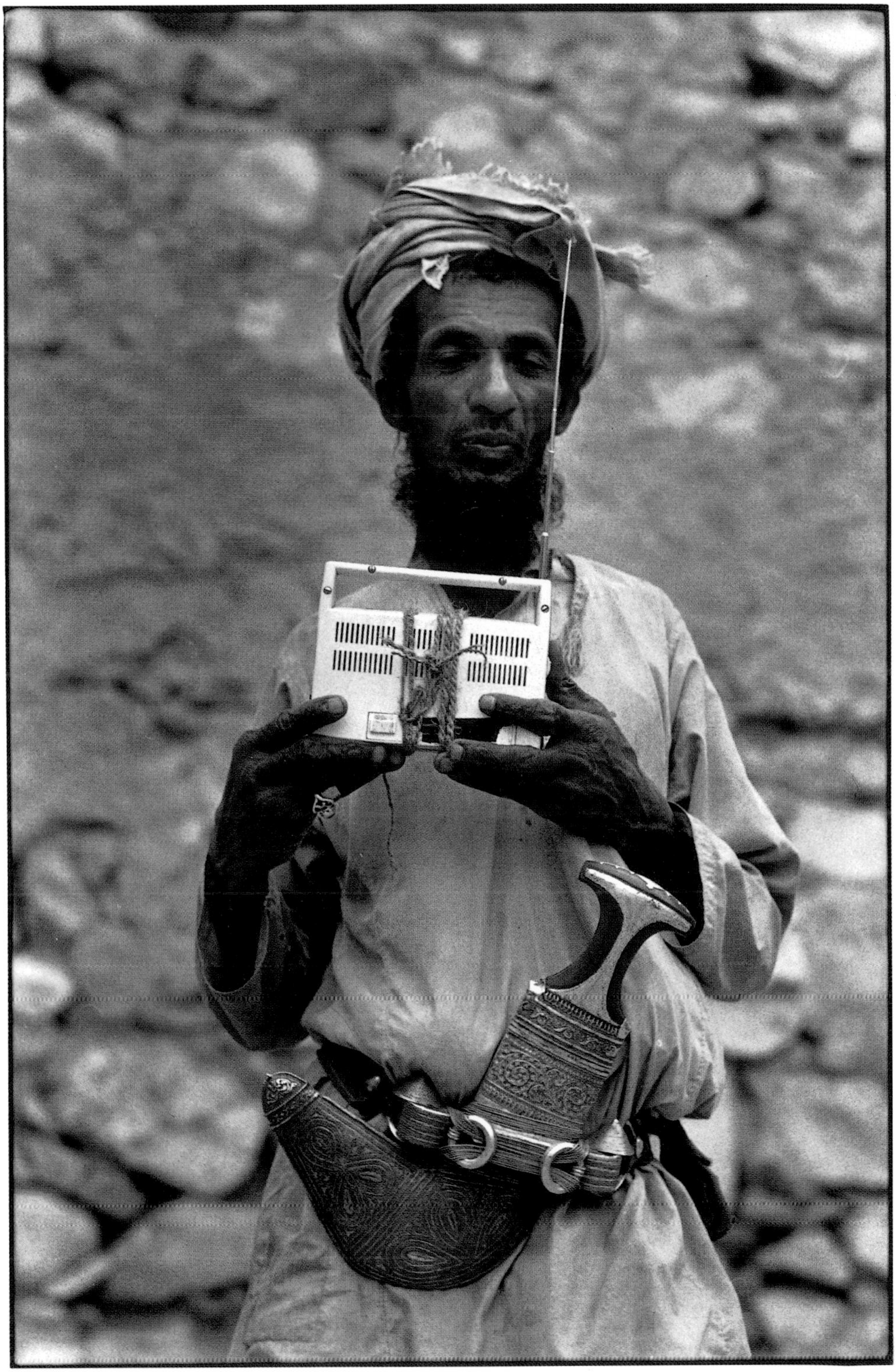

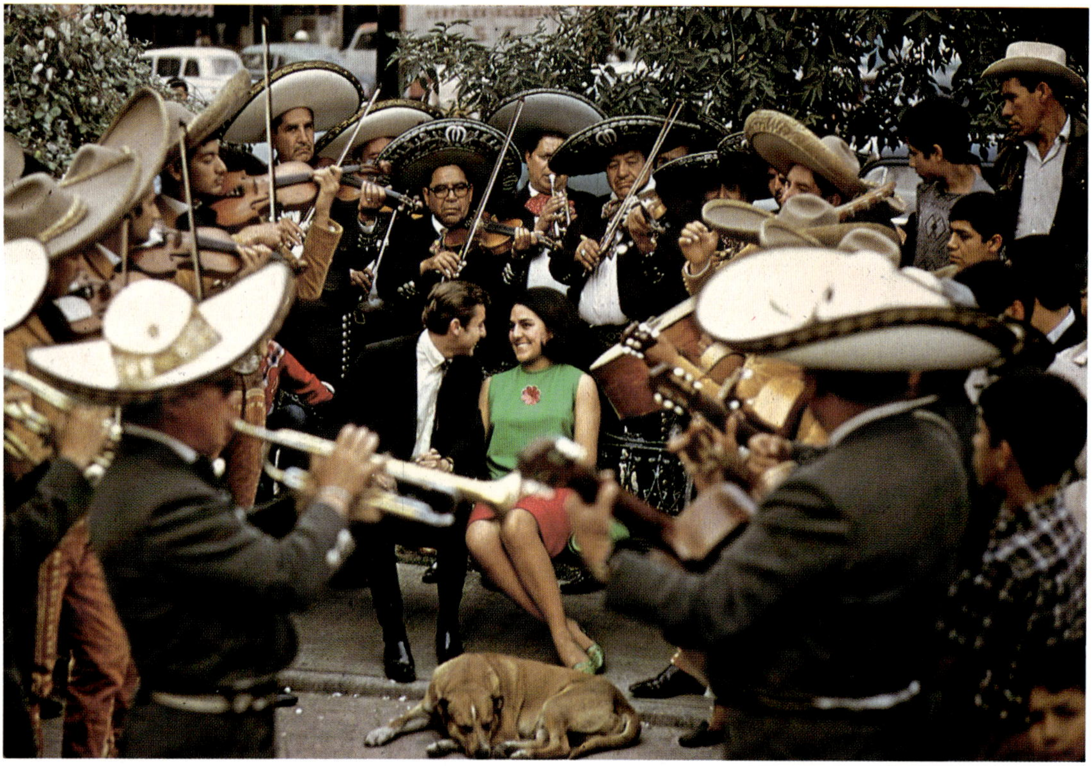

Thomas Hoepker
Mexico, 1967.

Inge Morath
Feria, Seville, 1974.

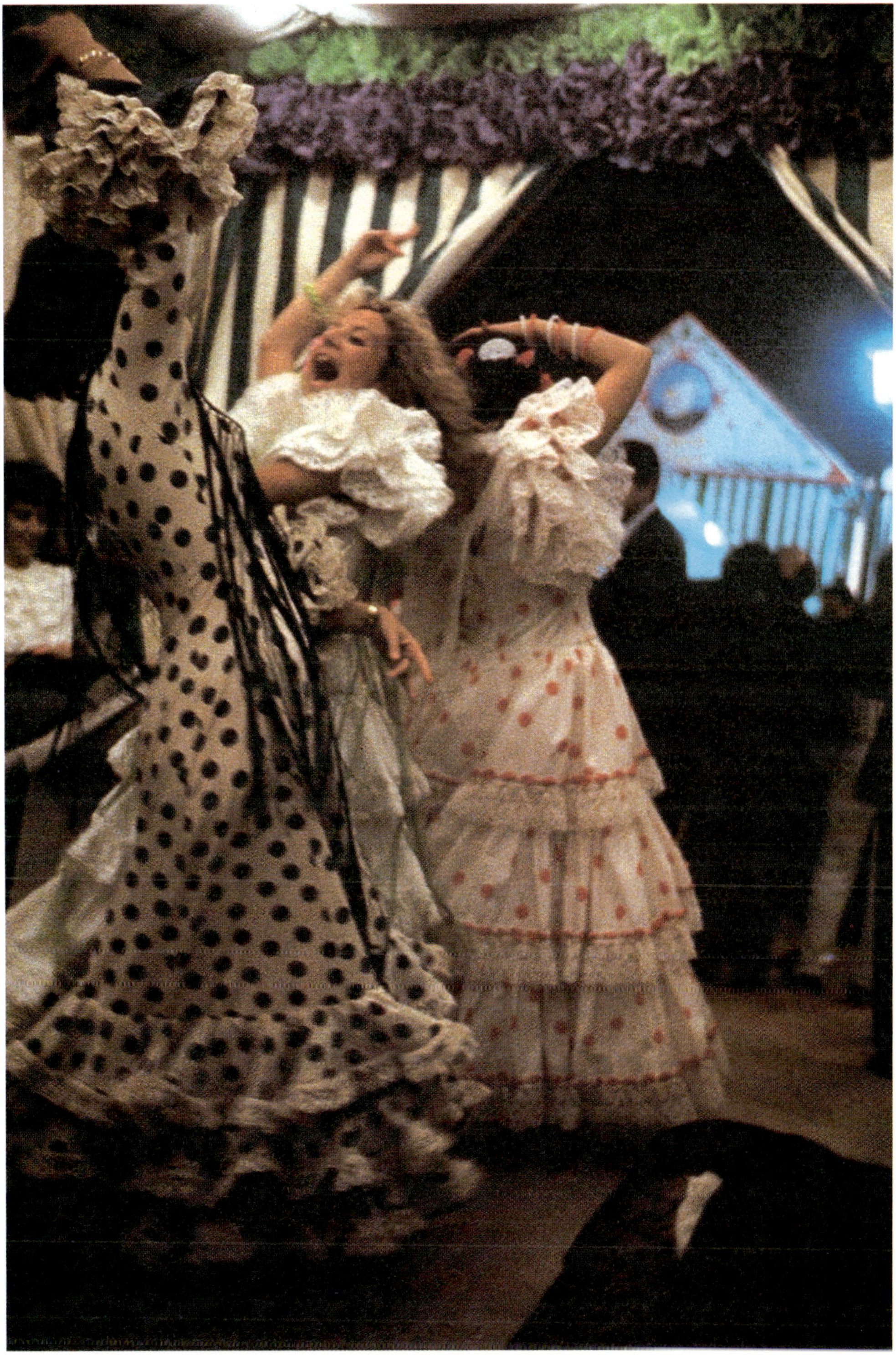

Magnum Images wishes to thank
Eve Arnold, Neil Burgess,
Chris Boot *and the library staffs of Magnum London, New York and Paris for their efforts in preparing 'Music'.*

Special thanks are due to **Belinda Rathbone** *for principal research in New York, and* **Patricia Stratherne** *in Paris.*

Art Director **Michael Rand**
Designer **Ian Denning**